DATE DUE

FIESTA OF SUNSET

THE PEACE CORPS, GUATEMALA AND A SEARCH FOR TRUTH

TAYLOR DIBBERT

iUNIVERSE, INC.
NEW YORK   BLOOMINGTON

Fiesta of Sunset
The Peace Corps, Guatemala and a Search for Truth

A portion of this work was previously published in Slow Trains Literary Journal.

iUniverse books may be ordered through booksellers or by contacting:

iUniverse
1663 Liberty Drive
Bloomington, IN 47403
www.iuniverse.com
1-800-Authors (1-800-288-4677)

Because of the dynamic nature of the Internet, any Web addresses or links contained in this book may have changed since publication and may no longer be valid.

ISBN: 978-1-4502-7222-3 (sc)
ISBN: 978-1-4502-7224-7 (dj)
ISBN: 978-1-4502-7223-0 (ebk)

Library of Congress Control Number: 2010916859

Printed in the United States of America

iUniverse rev. date: 3/29/2011

This book is lovingly dedicated to my grandmother, Ann Dibbert.

CONTENTS

PROLOGUE

"My task which I am trying to achieve is, by the power of the written word to make you hear, to make you feel—it is, before all, to make you see. That—and no more, and it is everything. If I succeed, you shall find there according to your deserts: encouragement, consolation, fear, charm—all you demand—and, perhaps, also that glimpse of truth for which you have forgotten to ask."

—*Joseph Conrad*

I grew up in the Park Cities, a wealthy Dallas neighborhood often disparagingly referred to as "the Bubble." Lots in the Bubble routinely sell for over one million dollars. Just the lot. The most common challenges faced by the police are underage drinking and speeding violations, and the schools are outstanding. In fact, Highland Park High School is one of the most prestigious public high schools in the country. I can say without hesitation that I received an excellent education and feel very blessed.

There is, however, a downside to growing up in the Bubble: I experienced little intellectual diversity and even less racial or cultural diversity. I learned more about the world elsewhere. To begin with, I grew up in a family of readers and a house full of books, thousands of them. And as a family, we traveled a lot, in the United States and overseas.

My parents are not globe-trotters, far from it. But they wanted me and my younger brother to see the world. They wanted us to understand the joy of learning about other cultures. They wanted to make sure we understood that Dallas Cowboys football, Texas barbecue, and country music were not the only things that mattered. And so I grew up reading, traveling, and exploring the world. And I learned to love the adventure of it all.

As an undergraduate at the University of Georgia, I began my own travels—first throughout the South, primarily during football season. I visited places like Knoxville, Baton Rouge, Tuscaloosa, Talladega, Auburn, Charlottesville, and a bunch of small towns in Georgia.

I also studied abroad, in Argentina, Austria, and Spain, stopping in many other countries along the way. I loved meeting new people and learning about different cultures; I loved learning about all kinds of things. And I realized that traveling and reading were the two best ways for me to learn. I began to read voraciously in college and have never stopped: Hemingway, Fitzgerald, Dostoyevsky, Conrad, Coetzee, and Hesse are some of my favorites. I read books on history, current affairs, philosophy, and travel. And of course, my education would have been incomplete without the *Economist* and the *Financial Times,* the world's two greatest newspapers. Yes, the *Economist* still considers itself a newspaper, not a magazine.

As in high school, my grades in college were mediocre. I graduated with a 2.94 GPA, the result of too many late nights in bars and not enough time in the library. I rarely went to class during my first three years in Athens, an obvious mistake. During my senior year, I finally decided to apply myself and it paid off. I even made a 4.0 my last semester. And so I started to think about my future. What would I do with a political science degree from the University of Georgia? Many political-science majors were off to law school in the fall, which never appealed to me. I always thought law school would be three years of boredom followed by a lifetime of boredom.

What else? I needed something different, something more peculiar, something more distinctive. I needed something that I really cared about. In the fall of 2004, after my Contemporary Political Thought class, I found my answer on a bulletin board in Terrell Hall. "Life is calling. How far will you go?" I saw a man—maybe it was a boy—standing on a dock, about to jump off. The sun was setting behind him. Then I noticed a circular red, white, and blue logo. And it dawned on me. That's the American flag. It was an ad for the Peace Corps. And I said to myself, *Why not?*

Applying to the Peace Corps is a long, tedious process. For me, that process began in the spring of 2004. In January of 2006, I received my official invitation package. The Peace Corps will not tell a Prospective Peace Corps volunteer (PCV) the country he has been invited to over the phone. The prospective do-gooder must wait for a letter in the mail. The applicant can always decline the invitation, but you never know if or when you'll be sent another. I had already decided that I would accept an invitation to any country as long as it was Spanish-speaking, although I was hoping for Peru or Ecuador. I have always been fascinated by the political, economic, and cultural history of those two countries.

My acceptance package was supposed to arrive around Christmas. At the time, I was in Italy with my family. During those two weeks in Italy, I never slept well, and I barely even remember what I did. I wanted to know. I needed to know. Where would I be spending the next twenty-seven months of my life? What type of job would I have? Would I like the work? Would I get homesick? Would I be able to make friends? Would I regret the decision?

When we returned to Dallas, I raced to the post office to pick up our mail. My official Peace Corps package had arrived. I waited until I was home to open it. I was going to Guatemala. I would start in May. I would be one of fifteen new Appropriate Technology Peace Corps volunteers. Some of the "technologies" we might build included rainwater catchment tanks, solar showers, stoves, water systems, and rope pumps. The Peace Corps said they couldn't exactly guarantee what I would be doing. The Peace Corps said I would spend my first three months in training and live with a host family. After two months in country, I would learn where I would be spending my next two years. The documents I received were full of ambiguity. I hardly understood my job assignment, but I accepted without hesitation. With a sense of pragmatic altruism, guarded optimism, humanitarian resolve, anxiety, fear, and a bit of courage, I decided to join the Peace Corps. Within a few months, I would call Guatemala my home.

This book is a chronicle of the twenty-seven months I spent in Guatemala, from May 2006 to August 2008. It has been difficult for me to write. I have always felt ambivalent about putting my thoughts and feelings into words. I have never wanted to share my imperfections with the world. I assumed that no one would understand me. That changed in Guatemala. I left the Peace Corps feeling no less flawed, but I no longer care. The twenty-nine other people in my training group and one shrewd Englishman showed me that I had nothing to fear, because I was not alone. They were a special group; they gave me the inspiration to finish my twenty-seven months of service. For that I will forever be grateful. This book is as much theirs as it is mine.

PART I

ONE: PRIOR TO DEPARTURE

"If you have built castles in the air, your work need not be lost; that is where they should be. Now put foundations under them."
—Henry David Thoreau

APRIL 2006: DALLAS

My departure is less than two weeks away, and I'm ready to begin the journey. There will be two days of "staging" in DC, and then I'm off to Guatemala for twenty-seven months. Right now I'm trying to get my mental house in order. From my previous journeys, I've learned that this is perhaps the most crucial component of successfully living and traveling abroad. Without some semblance of inner peace, I'll never turn a foreign land into my home. At this point, I think the adventure will be much more intellectual and spiritual than physical. To clarify: I have no doubt that the work will be physically challenging. I only mean to say that the greatest challenges and more significant personal growth will come from within.

I hope to write frequently while I'm in Guatemala. I believe books are such a personal thing. And the writing of those books is infinitely more personal. It's crazy to think that the vast majority of people who consume books and literature have never and will never meet those men and women who have given us a piece of their lives. To me, publishing a memoir would be analogous to walking around naked in an airport—not something I would feel comfortable doing. Hopefully one day I will have the courage to try, though I doubt it.

Mentally and physically, I'm as ready as I'll ever be, although deciding what to take with me is tough. The Peace Corps packing list sheds no light on an already opaque situation. Choosing which books to bring feels like I'm deciding which children are allowed to enter my ark before the flood, but decisions must be made. Hemingway, Dostoyevsky, Steinbeck, and Bret Easton Ellis have all made the cut. Fortunately, my dad has helped me put tons of music on my new iPod. Most surprisingly, I discovered my favorite pair of words only yesterday: solar adaptor. I guess even electricity is a luxury in Guatemala. God, how poor are these people?

MAY 1, 2006

Today is the big day: I'm heading to Washington DC, for "Peace Corps staging," a two-day orientation. There's no turning back now. I'm harboring a highly diverse basket of emotions this morning. Yeah, there's a nice mix of everything in there, which basically means that I'm nervous as hell. I slept for maybe twenty minutes last night. I stayed up and listened almost exclusively to "Naive Melody" by Talking Heads. I probably listened to that one song seventy times.

I can't remember ever being this nervous. Two years of my mid-twenties will be gone when I come back! That's enough time for me to get lost, find myself, and then lose myself all over again. Once every three months, approximately thirty new Peace Corps trainees fly to Guatemala City to begin their service. Statistically speaking, one third of those folks will quit early. Quitting early in Peace Corps vernacular is known as "ETing." ET stands for Early Termination. From what I hear, people choose to leave for all kinds of reasons—with the desire to be closer to significant others in the United States and homesickness being the two most common.

Joining the Peace Corps is the greatest risk that I have ever taken. There are so many unknowns, so many concerns of mine that have not been allayed. I have no idea how this will turn out. Right now, I can't even contemplate an Early Termination. I don't need a shameful black mark on my life story. But what if I am wrong? What if I fail? Would I be doomed to a life of failure? If I left early, I would be embarrassed. I would feel terrible. I don't want to go home with my tail between my legs. I don't want to quit because I couldn't handle it. I hope I'm tougher than that.

Will my time in the Peace Corps leave a lasting influence? Ernest Hemingway, a man for whom my respect continues undiminished, spoke of Paris being a "moveable feast." The time that he spent there in the 1920s, in his mid-twenties, had a lasting effect on him—both in terms of his career as a writer and his view of the world. I turn twenty-four in December. If I am lucky, Guatemala will become my "moveable feast." If I am lucky, I will encounter trials and tribulations that I will grow to embrace as significant rites of passage. If I am lucky, my time in the Peace Corps will leave an indelible mark on my life. If I am lucky, it will be an experience from which I can draw inspiration until I breathe my last breath.

MAY 2, 2006: WASHINGTON DC

Despite what any Peace Corps official may say, "staging" is a complete waste of everyone's time. Our group filled out pointless worksheets and participated in some childish role-play activities. On one occasion, each group of five was asked to draw a picture for everyone else. This picture was supposed to convey how we were feeling about moving to Guatemala. The group next to ours drew a picture of a guy jumping off a cliff and then landing in a pile of rocks. Pure poetry! They got a big laugh, but only because that picture rang true in everyone's heart and mind. I can't believe

I'm sitting around with twenty-nine people who have also joined the Peace Corps! None of us has any idea what we're getting into. Of that there can be no doubt.

MAY 3, 2006: DULLES INTERNATIONAL AIRPORT, WASHINGTON DC

I use the airport bathroom near our departure gate. I slowly sip from a water fountain nearby. I have not yet realized that water fountains are a luxury. I buy a copy of today's *Wall Street Journal*. I flash my fancy Peace Corps passport. I board the plane. This is it. Fellow Peace Corps trainee Andrew Gall from New Hampshire sits across the aisle.

"Hey fella, what are you thinking?"

"Not much, Taylor. I just a second ago realized that this is it. There's no way to avoid it now. I'm going to Guatemala."

Both of us are now laughing.

"You are right about that, Andrew. We should be all right though."

We're interrupted by the voice of the pilot. "Good morning, ladies and gentlemen.... Once we reach a cruising altitude of thirty-six thousand feet, we'll go ahead and turn off the seat-belt sign.... I'd also like to say that it's an honor to have thirty members of the Peace Corps traveling with us. We certainly wish them well; we know they will be doing a lot of good work down in Guatemala."

Wow. As dumb as it sounds, his words kind of choke me up. Then, suddenly, out of nowhere, I hear something, a smooth crescendo. The entire plane, nearly a full house, is applauding. At that moment, I feel like I am part of something special. I feel special—regular old me. Could this really be happening?

Two: In Country

May 3, 2006

We arrive in Guatemala City and sluggishly deplane. Everyone looks exhausted, and we haven't even done anything yet. It is hot. I've been in Guatemala for less than ten minutes, and I'm already sweating profusely. I use the bathroom and restively wait for my luggage like everybody else.

We've just been greeted by the Peace Corps country director, Cynthia Threlkeld, and the training director, Craig Badger. Now we are leaving the airport to meet the host families with whom we will live during our three months of Peace Corps training in Santa Lucía Milpas Altas, which is just outside of Antigua. Actually, Santa Lucía Milpas Altas is where the training center is, but members from my training group will live in several towns besides Santa Lucía—La Libertad, Santo Tomás, and Magdalena, all in the department of Sacatepéquez. Departments in Guatemala are similar to states in the United States, and there are twenty-two in all. I never did get to know Ms. Threlkeld; she left to pursue a job in Africa shortly after my group arrived in country. I think she was offered a Peace Corps directorship there.

An hour later, I discover that where I'll be living is not that bad. There's even a showerhead in the bathroom—I had been bracing myself for bucket baths during training. In my bedroom, I have an electrical outlet *and* a chair. I'm living like a king in this Mayan paradise. I exchange pleasantries with the host family, but it's been a long day. I'm ready to pop a couple of Tylenol PMs and hit the sack, which is exactly what I do.

I have ambitiously planned to drink five cups of coffee before training starts tomorrow. About five years ago, I discovered that coffee is one of life's great pleasures, and now I cannot imagine my life without it. I love the way it smells, even though the taste is never as good as the aroma. I enjoy the taste of it, sure. But it's the caffeine that makes coffee so magical. It will course through my veins yet again tomorrow. I have been separated from my French press for only three days, and I am starting to feel uneasy. I didn't bring it with me because I thought my host family would think I'm weird or pretentious. Besides, I guess I could always buy one in Guatemala City or Antigua before I move to my site at the end of July. I remain guardedly optimistic about this; I have been told that Guatemalans export almost all of their good coffee.

Maybe I'll sleep well knowing that I don't have to deal with superficialities tomorrow. I won't have to listen to blowhards like Lou Dobbs on cable television either. Partisan grandstanding has become synonymous with purportedly logical solutions to my nation's energy crisis. The November election can't come soon enough.

I will remember for the rest of my life the day my Peace Corps journey became official. My dad was driving me to Dallas/Fort Worth International Airport, and we saw the deluge of traffic coming into Dallas. Everybody heading into the city was just stuck. As we drove along, I sat ruminating in the passenger seat. "I'm not sure what I'm getting myself into, but thank God it isn't *that.*" Monotonous white-collar jobs, dull cubicles, marriage, and kids are not going anywhere. Dallas is not going anywhere. So I'll cling to the goddess of youth—a fleeting deity if there ever was one. More importantly, I will try to help someone besides myself;

I have seen enough of the world to know that I have been given enough help.

MAY 4, 2006

The coffee I drink this morning at my new home in Santo Tomás is terrible, basically a cheap version of Nescafé. I would later discover that Nescafé is the most expensive brand of instant coffee. Most Guatemalans only drink instant coffee. Over breakfast, I ask my host mom if she knows what a French press is. She tells me that she has never been to France.

Our first day of training begins at the training center, located in Santa Lucía Milpas Altas. Santa Lucía is a modest town situated between Antigua and Guatemala City. All the trainees are huddled in a circle with Country Director Cynthia Threlkeld. Until now, I had not known that Guatemala is, in fact, a popular and desired destination for Peace Corps volunteers. Ms. Threlkeld might be lying; the place had always seemed culturally bland to me. But she gives a decent spiel.

Evidently, our training group is comprised of two separate program groups: Small Business Development and Appropriate Technology. There are fifteen people in each group. Peace Corps volunteers do all kinds of work in Guatemala, including projects pertaining to small business, municipal development, agriculture, environmental issues, health, education, and infrastructure development. The Appropriate Technology program is focused primarily on building "technologies" to help rural families. Examples of these technologies would include ferro-cement tanks that capture rainwater, family stoves that conserve wood and channel smoke outside the home, and gravity-flow water systems. Water-system construction normally entails running PVC pipe from an isolated spring site to a distribution tank and then on to households.

MAY 5, 2006

Our formal Peace Corps medical briefings have begun. The head nurse, Kathy Arroyave, discusses some of the salient health issues in the country along with other medical policies and procedures of Peace Corps Guatemala.

"Okay guys, can anybody tell me what the most common health problem is among Peace Corps volunteers in Guatemala?"

Nobody speaks for at least a minute. I think all of us realize that this is a great time to space out.

"All right. Nobody knows? Okay, well, last year a hundred and seventeen cases of diarrhea were diagnosed for every hundred volunteers in the country."

Everyone laughs. Then we all realize that those numbers must be distorted. I'm sure plenty of people don't call the medical office when they have a bad case of the runs. In fact, who would ever call the medical office when they have the runs? What a bunch of weaklings. That's ridiculous. My mind starts to wander. What constitutes official diarrhea anyway?

For those of you who are wondering, *diarrhea* means that someone has four consecutive bowel movements that are inconsistent or watery. That is the technical definition of diarrhea in Peace Corps Guatemala.

Today we also discuss more safety and security policies, conduct Spanish interviews (to place people in classes according to ability), and receive the official training schedule. I never imagined the Peace Corps could be so boring. Of course, I've never had a real job, so I have nothing to compare it with. Later on, a group of current volunteers speak with us so that we can get the other side of the story. During the Peace Corps volunteer panel, the administration is not allowed in the room. Thank God.

Apparently, last year, one of the rape incidents was not included in the safety statistics presented to us yesterday. The following is supposedly a true story and one that I don't want to believe.

A female volunteer was raped. She was out "late at night." No one could be exactly sure what hour that was. The Peace Corps administration concluded that it was her fault for putting herself at risk by staying out late. She was summarily sent home. The details of this story are sketchy, largely due to the fact that she did not come forward with the rape charge until several weeks after the incident occurred.

We heard another story about four PCVs who were kicked out recently. With a good deal of liquid courage, they tried to scale the main church in Panajachel, Sololá. Even though only two of them were caught scaling the church wall, all four were put on a plane back to the United States. It was guilt by association, which seems grossly unfair. And to think that this was the same night they were sworn in and became official Peace Corps volunteers!

MAY 7, 2006

This morning, the medical staff gives all trainees a copy of *Where There is No Doctor: A Village Health Care Handbook*. If I read even one page of that book, I will subconsciously induce some strange and potentially lethal illness. Under the most extreme circumstances, the book might be relevant if I were stranded in a remote African village. But I did not join the Peace Corps to serve as a midwife. I did not come here to figure out what kind or rash I've got, nor did I come here to study epidemiology. Under no circumstances do I feel like getting in touch with my psychosomatic side.

In many ways, training is similar to elementary school. Every day, my host mother, Ana Lucrecia, prepares my lunch. Then I walk for about forty-five minutes, lunch pail in hand, to Santa Lucía. Usually I meet some of my fellow trainees at the park in Santo Tomás beforehand. Then we walk to the "school," or Peace Corps training center, together.

I review this routine as I relax in my bedroom. I also discover that my bedroom looks like a toolshed and smells like a barn. Maybe having the bathroom nearby should not be viewed as a convenience.

I have been in country for less than a week, but I'm already exhausted. I lie on my bed fully clothed, but I still feel somewhat exposed. I feel vulnerable and defenseless in an ethereal, intangible sort of way. My life has never felt more tenuous. I have taken a leap with twenty-nine other people. I have committed to the Peace Corps, but I have no idea what I'm doing. My site assignment is still unclear, because site assignments aren't given until the end of June. So until the end of June I don't even know where my new home will be. This is frustrating. I have been told that Peace Corps training is vastly different from Peace Corps service, although the differences are still unclear. How am I supposed to prepare? Why is the process so ambiguous?

MAY 8, 2006: SANTO TOMÁS

This afternoon I meet Eric Black, a loquacious and tubby Peace Corps volunteer. Eric stayed at Ana Lucrecia's house during his training. He has decided to pay her a visit today since he had a meeting in Guatemala City this morning. So far, Eric is the fattest PCV I have come across. He's also the most long-winded. However, it is hard to reject the guy, because he is so friendly.

"Well good afternoon, sir. I'm Eric. I actually lived here two years ago. Yep, almost exactly two years ago I was right where you are now. What's my point? Oh, right. So how are you getting along here in Santo Tomás?"

"Fine. I just got here last week. I can't complain."

"Okay, well, great. Welcome aboard, my good man. It's quite a ride down here with the old *Cuerpo de Paz*. It's good stuff, though. I truly have enjoyed my time here. You know, I even have a nice little Guatemalan girlfriend. Yeah, we've been dating for around six months now. I'd say things are going pretty well. I'm out in San Marcos. Do you know where that is? What'd you say your name was, by the way?"

"Taylor. I don't know where San Marcos is."

This guy is so verbose. I begin to wonder if he's serious. I'd be shocked if he has any close friends down here. He's too talkative.

I'm scared of opening those floodgates another time; he might never stop speaking. Already, Eric has lost me in his impenetrable jungle of verbal communication. Yet I am curious. Eric's got to know something that can help me. He must possess some useful knowledge. Ambivalently, I decide to press on.

"How did you like training, Eric?"

"I liked it all right, buddy—just be careful about all the *chisme*. It can get pretty crazy sometimes."

"*Chisme*. The gossip? What do you mean?"

"You haven't heard? Oh boy, you sure are green. Here's the deal: be careful about what you say and to whom you say it. Since you're a trainee, they are watching you at all times. I kid you not, sir."

"They?"

Now the guy has piqued my interest.

"You bet, buddy. I'm talking about the teachers, the trainers, the country director, and the training director, all of them. They're always checking you guys out. You didn't know?"

"No, though I appreciate the heads-up. It sounds like gossip is the official sport of Peace Corps Guatemala."

"Haha! You're funny, man. No problem. I'm happy to do it. I was once in your shoes."

Eric looks excited; he must have an anecdote coming.

"I remember back when I was a trainee almost exactly two years ago, I got into an argument with our host mom. It was some stupid teacher's fault. I got back from training one day, and Ana Lucrecia just plain called me out."

"What do you mean, Eric?"

"She called me out for not eating all of her home-cooked food during lunch. It's just nuts. Look at me. Look at how overweight I am. I'm twenty or thirty pounds overweight. I eat everything. At the training center for lunch, I ate tons of food, just tons of it really. I'll tell you what I think happened, buddy."

"Okay."

"What happened is that somebody caught me sharing a little of my lunch. But what's wrong with that? I mean, it's just crazy to think that somebody would care. I thought it was no big deal. Anyways, you just got to be careful. The same goes with partying. You get me?"

"Partying?"

"Oh, sure. There's always a solid group of drinkers. It happens with every training group. If you're one of the party people, if you get that reputation, they know about it for sure. You'll be on the radar for two years, if you last that long."

"The radar?"

"You bet. The radar. You want to be off the administration's radar. Keep that in mind when you go out drinking with your buddies. It may catch up with you if you aren't careful."

"Well, okay. It was good meeting you, man. If I don't see you before you finish your service …"

"Finish my service? You'll run into me again for sure, buddy. Didn't I tell you that I'm extending?"

"Oh, really?"

"It probably has something to do with that nice little Guatemalan girlfriend of mine. Yep, I just re-upped for a whole year extension. Anyways, I'll see you around, buddy."

"Sure man, later."

As Eric heads out the front gate, I consider what he has said. That jovial guy did have some good points. I had not heard of the administration's radar until now. I figured there would be some gossip, largely due to extreme boredom among volunteers, but I never figured it would be too big a deal. He has lived here for two years; he must know some things.

THE POLITICS OF TYRANNY

I'm learning a lot about Guatemalan history and politics in my Spanish class. At times, Guatemalan history can be overwhelming. Basically, the country has been hopelessly mired in poverty and corruption since the early nineteenth century, when it first became an independent country. I feel like I have been given a Peace Corps assignment in the coup d'état capital of the world. I have lost some respect for Ronald Reagan, just as I have lost some respect for Margaret Thatcher. I guess the Iron Lady forgot about Guatemala when she said that Ronald Reagan had defeated the Soviet Union without firing a shot. In reality, Reagan fired a lot of shots in Central America, albeit indirectly. The US government financed proxy wars in Latin America and Africa throughout the Cold War. During Guatemala's thirty-six-year civil war, experts estimate that 200,000 people were killed. The vast majority of those people were indigenous. The Reagan administration gave Guatemala's military regime hundreds of millions of dollars during the 1980s without even blinking.

The modern era of Latin American oppression started back in 1954 during Dwight D. Eisenhower's presidency. Fresh off a "successful" coup in Iran a year earlier, the American government decided to try their luck closer to home. After all, if the United States could manipulate a country like Iran, an insignificant piece of real estate in Central America should be a piece of cake.

The target was social liberal and democratically elected Jacobo Arbenz. Arbenz had instituted a Law of Agrarian Reform in 1952. Under the new law, the Guatemalan government was to buy approximately four hundred thousand acres of unused United Fruit Company land for a fair market value. This worried United Fruit and other US business interests in Guatemala. Arbenz's attempts at land reform coupled with his outspoken advocacy of indigenous rights convinced the US government that he was a communist.

The 1954 military coup that overthrew Arbenz was led by the CIA and may have been the biggest American foreign policy mistake of the twentieth century. It was a seminal moment in both American and Guatemalan history. The US government had started to think these coups could be pulled off without a hitch and that they were easy. In fact, the 1961 Bay of Pigs fiasco was modeled after the Guatemalan coup.

It's hard to believe that two brothers held the position of secretary of state and CIA director at the same time. And both brothers had significant links to the United Fruit Company. That sounds like a hypothetical scenario out of an Orwell novel. The 1954 coup generated a period of heightened violence and oppression in the country. The Guatemalan people would know nothing but military dictatorships until the UN-sponsored peace accords were signed in 1996. To this day, there is no compelling historical evidence that proves Jacobo Arbenz was a communist, or that he had been influenced by the Soviet Union. That's because he wasn't a communist, and the Soviets weren't interested in Guatemala. In reality, the Soviets never tried to gain influence in the country.

MAY 9, 2006

I lie on my bed and feel sorry for myself. My day has not gone all that smoothly. Yesterday I had the runs, but now I think I have taken too much Pepto-Bismol. Or maybe I still haven't taken enough. I have been queasy and bloated for the last twenty-four hours. I'm also feeling a little uncomfortable because nearly everyone in my project group seems to have actual construction experience, and I have none. I am anxious to *do* something instead of listening to the trainers ramble on about hypothetical work projects.

I get up to wander around. As I walk through the house, I take note of my host family's living conditions for the first time. The four kids share a tiny room. The girls share one small bed; the two boys get the other. I have mixed feelings about children. I get along with kids fairly well. However, the older I get, the more they scare me. I guess this is because some of my friends in the United States have already started families of their own. I'm not ready to be a father. The idea terrifies me.

I have been told that the families that house Peace Corps volunteers are not that poor. Nevertheless, they are still quite poor by American standards. I have never been this close to poverty before. As an avid traveler, I always looked upon the world's poor from a more voyeuristic, distant perspective. This is different. This is Peace Corps.

And frankly, these people would not be housing Peace Corps volunteers if they didn't need the money. I'm not making their lives any easier. I'm an inconvenience. Jerónimo, my host father, has to work two jobs in separate cities. Ana Lucrecia told me that he helps out in the kitchen in some fancy hotel in the capital and also works for the post office in Antigua. The guy is rarely home. And when he is, he treats me like I'm the one in charge, which can be a bit awkward at times. Ana Lucrecia has her hands full during the day. She cooks for everyone, including me. Typically, she will ride the *camioneta* (a chicken bus) from her house to Santa Lucía Milpas Altas and deliver me my lunch at around noon. Their four kids are adorable. Ruby is the youngest and by far the most inquisitive. Most Guatemalans hold a vastly different view of privacy than Americans; the issue is handled far more delicately in the United States. If my door isn't locked, Ruby will barge in unannounced, sit on my bed, and start asking me questions. "How are you, Taylor? What are you doing, Taylor? What are you doing tomorrow, Taylor? Do you miss your family in the US? Where did you learn to speak Spanish?" Ruby is tireless, though it's hard to ever be frustrated with her. She is only a child, maybe seven or eight years old.

The older daughter, Cindy is far less curious. She is fourteen. Her facial features are almost identical to Ana Lucrecia's; for now, that is where the similarities end. Cindy is tall for her age and quite thin, while her mother is built like a beach ball with stubby legs. Ana Lucrecia is probably four-and-a-half feet tall, though she must be at least sixty pounds overweight. This makes sense. I've yet to see her walk more than a few feet at once. She is always working around the house—cooking, washing clothes, cleaning. Like most Guatemalan women, Ana Lucrecia works hard. Her day never seems to end.

The two boys are much more reticent around me. Melvin is fifteen, and I think Kevin is ten. Both of the boys dress like Americans, and I have begun to realize why. Many of the clothes worn by Guatemalans are gifts from the United States. On my way to the training center yesterday, I saw a guy wearing a Dallas Cowboys sweatshirt and another man wearing a Michael Jordan T-shirt. Americans donating clothing would explain this. That's not the only reason, either. Used American clothing is sold throughout Guatemala; these places that sell *ropa Americana* are known as PACA stores. Of course, in the indigenous villages, it would only be the men who would dress this way. All the women still wear *traje*—the traditional indigenous clothing.

I have just realized how American-sounding all their names are: Melvin, Kevin, Cindy, and Ruby. These names are probably more common in Minnesota than in Guatemala. But I would quickly learn that classic American names are quite popular here. I have also just realized the importance of the word *pues* ("well") in Guatemalan Spanish. These *Chapines* ("Guatemalans") use the word all the time. "Have a nice day, *pues. Pues*, I don't know what the answer is, *pues. Pues*, wait one minute. *Pues*, that's fine. Yes, *pues. Pues* … no. *Pues, Pues, Pues, Pues, Pues*." I probably hear the word *pues* about twenty times at day. This means that I will have heard the word *pues* approximately two thousand times by the time I finish training. If I make it through two years of service, I will have heard the word *pues* around fifteen thousand times. Admittedly, my calculations are imprecise. I am not sure where I'll be living after training, nor what the *pues* to words that are not *pues* ratio will be at my future site. I already hate this word.

MAY 11, 2006

Politically speaking, most Peace Corps volunteers lean far to the left. This is no secret. I have already been told that I am one of less than ten Republicans currently serving in Peace Corps Guatemala. Right now, there are nearly two hundred volunteers in country. I'm no staunch conservative, but I was raised in a very conservative household in a very conservative state. A part of my personality is naturally a reflection of my upbringing. I stand out among my fellow trainees; I bring a different perspective to the table.

I also stand out for another reason: I have not brought a Nalgene water bottle to Guatemala. I now believe that I have been placed in a Peace Corps training group with the world's most serious water drinkers. I think I'm the only person who didn't bring one of those water bottles down here. A couple of people have already told me they've brought more than one. Lord. That's intense. And these are not small, discreet bottles, either. These are bottles that would last me at least a half a day.

At the training center, everyone eats lunch on benches in the courtyard. The weather today couldn't be better—clear skies and a light breeze. I am sitting at a table with fellow trainees Andrew Gall and a female who will remain anonymous. Not surprisingly, today's conversation turns political. It's ironic that the Peace Corps prides itself on being apolitical—officially, that is. I understand why the US government must take this stance. Nevertheless, most of the members of my training group seek to ardently debate political or foreign-policy issues whenever possible. Today would be no exception.

"Bush really could be compared to Hitler. I mean, not in all ways, but in some ways."

"You can't be serious. I mean, I'm not a huge Bush fan, but I was a history major. I am quite certain that you can't compare him to Hitler."

I decide to let Andrew and our female companion talk it out a little more before I say anything.

"But look at all that oppression, guys, and he should be tried for war crimes, and he has been responsible for the death of millions if not billions, and it's just about oil and all the corporations, but mostly about American imperialism and that stuff."

"Okay, look, I'm just not sure that Bush is comparable to Hitler. It sounds silly if you just think about it."

"Whatever, man, I just think that people should stand up to the neoconservatives and those ruthless multinational corporations. I just think our country should be ashamed of itself. I think we should be ashamed to be Americans until we get out of Iraq. Do you two really not agree with that?"

Finally, I am ready to jump in. This could be fun.

"Listen, lady. If you are so ashamed of the United States, why are you representing the US abroad as a Peace Corps volunteer? Shouldn't you be doing something else? You aren't making a whole lot of sense."

"How can you say that? People just want peace. They just want to end the oppression. Bush never should have gotten into Harvard Business School. He's an idiot."

Obviously, this girl is ill-equipped to deal with the voice of reason. Frankly, I'm wondering if she's stoned, but I probably shouldn't ask this question at the training center. Of course, drug use is strictly prohibited in Peace Corps Guatemala.

"What are you talking about? Just answer my question. How can you hate America and then represent that same country abroad? How can you be the face of America if you hate our country?"

Andrew decides to chime in. "He does have a point, I suppose."

Amazingly, the tide has turned in my favor.

"Whatever, guys. You guys can just deal with it. I just think we should end this war, and there's no better way to do that than to spread the peace. Peace Corps means peace, not US Army, not WMDs, not preemptive strikes but peace. I can't believe you guys even signed up."

Dumbfounded, Andrew and I can't help staring at this dogmatic and irrational chick. I realize that not all foreign-policy debate revolves around rational thought in a rational universe, but this is just nuts. So I shift my focus to finishing my fried eggs and refried beans. I follow that with a few more corn tortillas. I ignore the girl and save my opinions for another day. I know there are more like her in Guatemala, crazies lying in wait.

"All right, lady, whatever you say."

It's one o'clock. Lunch is over. The afternoon training session has just begun, and the three of us are late.

MAY 13, 2006

My relaxing Saturday afternoon is spent on the porch rereading Bret Easton Ellis's *Glamorama*. Normally I prefer to read inside so that I'm not bothered. Today I can't. It's such a beautiful day, I feel like it would be awkward if I just hid in my bedroom.

Ellis is one of my favorite authors. His satirical style is so unique, and he's always on point with his social commentary. Ellis believes we live in a dynamic yet shallow world, and that people can get caught up in trivialities without realizing it. I agree with him. Just pondering that exhausts me as I fall asleep in a plastic chair. Maybe an hour later, I am awakened by a hard rain. Still half asleep, I gaze upward at a blackened sky and hurry inside with my paperback. The Guatemalan rainy season has arrived.

Typically the wettest months of the year are from May through August or September. Never in my life have I seen so much rain. Now a bunch of us are hanging out at the local bar across from the training center, passing the time and enjoying a few beers. I did not think anyone was drinking that much. The bar is euphemistically referred to as "the library." The Peace Corps administrative staff will eventually find out that most of us are heavy drinkers; we might as well enjoy a brief grace period. At our table, we are mostly talking sports. At a table behind ours, a few of my fellow trainees are discussing anything but sports.

"So how many guys have you all slept with?"

"Don't you mean girls?"

"Okay, like, whatever."

"It's not like I'm keeping track. Isn't that kind of a personal question?"

"I've slept with nineteen people. I'm pretty sure I'm not a lesbian, though. I haven't had sex in four years either."

My goodness, this girl is a firecracker. I'm wondering if I misheard some of that. Peace Corps volunteers are not known for being timid or shy, but I cannot believe what I am hearing. I could drink all day and still not be this candid with my fellow trainees. I met these people less than two weeks ago. It's too early to be sharing secrets. I feel like there's already a lot of sexual tension in the group, and this is not going to help. I'm ready to walk home for dinner, and that's exactly what I do.

MAY 16, 2006

Today the medical staff conducts preliminary interviews. This is confusing to me, because I already turned in about twelve hundred pages of medical documents during the application process. I stroll into the office at one in the afternoon to answer some routine questions. At first everything is going fine. Then we turn to alcohol consumption.

"Okay, Taylor, and do you smoke?"

"No."

"Really, never?"

"I smoked marijuana several times in college."

"Okay, but I'm talking about cigarettes."

"Oh, then no."

"Okay, how many alcoholic drinks do you consume per week?"

Oh God. I try not to panic. I quickly decide to give her a reasonable number, a number lower than the truth. I am a recovering University of Georgia undergraduate. I just left college a few months ago.

"I'd say about … twenty … to thirty … drinks per week."

"Really?"

"Well, no, yes, but maybe closer to twenty than thirty usually."

"That's a lot of alcohol. Does alcoholism run in your family?"

"No, well, not that I know of. I mean, I don't think anyone in my family has been a clinical alcoholic. My grandfather abused alcohol, but that was a long time ago. Come to think of it, I did have an uncle who was a heavy drinker."

"Okay, thanks Taylor."

Head Nurse Kathy Arroyave is assiduously writing a bunch of stuff down as I exit. What is she writing? I'm an idiot. Why did I have to be so honest? I leave the room a mental wreck, but I cannot complain. This is entirely my fault.

MAY 19, 2006

I restively lie awake and beg for sleep to find me. I can hear rats scampering around the makeshift ceiling above my bed. It sounds like there are a lot of them up there. The scampering sounds like it's gotten too close. I hit the light switch just to be sure. I know I could be wrong, but not this time. I'm so freaked out that I'm out of suitable adjectives to describe the moment. I quickly jump out of my bed and am standing on my chair a second later. The rat is crawling down the wall adjacent to my bed. He is a healthy-looking fella; it looks like this rat gets more to eat than some of the people living in Santo Tomás. Three seconds later, the rat is on my bed. Fantastic. My heart is pounding, and there will be no sleep for me tonight. I greet the following morning with frustration and leave the house exhausted, looking haggard with bags under my eyes. The walk to Santa Lucía Milpas Altas that normally takes me forty-five minutes takes me more than an hour today.

MAY 20, 2006

I sleep well tonight. However, my innards must not have gotten much sleep. I frantically try to air my bedroom out before my host mom enters. I can barely breathe. The room smells like a giant rotten egg; I must have been farting all night. Never mind that, my room smells like a soiled diaper. Ana has noticed the stench—I can tell by the look on her face. I am embarrassed.

MAY 27, 2006: SATURDAY

We don't have to be at the training center this afternoon. Thank God. I'm starting to get sick of that place. Trainees are required to be at the training center from 7:30 a.m. to 4:00 p.m. Monday through Friday without exception. Peace Corps training is sometimes more tedious than middle school. As of now, we are not even allowed to spend a night away from our host family's house. We have been told that the average age of PCVs in Guatemala is twenty-seven, yet we are being treated like children.

I head to the capital with a few other trainees to watch *The Da Vinci Code* in English. The movie is disappointing. I don't think reading the book helped. Later on, we grab a few beers at Hooters. Yes, Hooters. And of course, the waitresses have certain "talents." The more I travel, the more I realize one cannot escape some of the tackier aspects of American culture.

We have a few pitchers of Gallo, the mediocre national beer of Guatemala, and then leave for Santo Tomás and our host families. Drinking in the capital is tough on a Peace Corp trainee stipend. Right now, they're giving us less than ten American dollars per week. I feel like most of the trainees have already started to use money from home.

MAY 28, 2006: PACAYA

Guatemala is home to more than thirty volcanoes, including Tajamulco, the highest point in Central America. I have heard that many PCVs are avid hikers, and many people make a concerted effort to climb a dozen volcanoes or more during their service.

Today I will hike Pacaya, a beautiful volcano situated approximately twenty miles south of Guatemala City, with three other PCVs. The four of us get picked up in Santo Tomás at 5:00 a.m. The van takes us right to the park, where we pay our entrance fee and start our climb. We are in a group of about twenty. We have one guide and a pair of armed escorts—these men are on horseback, and each has a shotgun. In spite of the additional security, we have been advised to leave all valuables behind. In Guatemala, tourists are occasionally robbed while climbing volcanoes. The guide forces us to stop every twenty minutes. This is for travelers who have only been in the country for a few days. Pacaya is a small volcano, but it still lies over eight thousand feet above sea level. It's obvious that most of the people we are hiking with have not yet adjusted to the change in elevation. Everyone is sucking wind except the four of us. It's a relatively easy climb, and we reach the summit after an hour and a half.

It's a beautiful, clear day. Visibility could not be better. We are free to walk around the crater for thirty minutes before we head back down. Pacaya has been active since the mid-1960s. I knew this, though I did not expect to see so much molten lava. This is cool. It's something that would never be allowed in the United States. I am inches away from flowing lava. I accidentally burn one of my shoes. A few clever people have brought marshmallows. What a great idea it was to come up here!

THREE: PEACE CORPS TRAINING

EARLY JUNE 2006

Training has gotten more intense; we are busy every day. This week, I have studied gravity-flow water systems, conducted water surveys for two days, and built an *estufa mejorada* with a couple other trainees. An *estufa mejorada* is just a simple stove made of bricks and mortar. Then we built some block latrines together. I never thought I could be such a handyman. I am learning by doing. Yet I am still wondering, what have I gotten myself into?

I have been in Guatemala only a month. Yet already there are things I miss from the United States. I miss red wine, friends and family, reputable international newspapers, and solid bowel movements. I still feel like I landed in country yesterday; at this point, I should not be missing anything too much. Strangely, a burst of homesickness hits me. I will learn to love Guatemala. It may even feel like home someday. It is hard to articulate my affection for the United States. My departure a month ago was confusing. I love my country, yet at times I don't know why. There is no appropriate word or group of words to describe a nation where a woman like Nancy Pelosi can be third in line for the presidency.

This morning I built a stove in La Libertad with three other people in my Appropriate Technology group. Today was the quintessential Peace Corps day. Right after we finished the base of our stove, the rain started to come down nonstop. We were short on supplies and forgot to bring a tarp to cover our work. Our stove was ruined after thirty minutes of angry rain. We would be forced to start from scratch the following morning. I was so frustrated; I wanted to throw a cement block through the window behind me.

JUNE 17, 2006

This morning I give a *charla,* or health talk, in front of my Appropriate Technology group on the subject of respiratory illnesses in Guatemala. I am the first one out of fifteen to present, and I feel that I did quite well. This is the big final project for my program. All fifteen of us must give an individual twenty-minute presentation in Spanish and then receive feedback from peers and Peace Corps administrators. I minored in Spanish in college, and having studied abroad in Spain and Argentina, this wasn't too big a deal for me. Conversely, for people who arrived in Guatemala with little or no Spanish, this is a stressful assignment.

MID-JUNE 2006

The second field-based training in Huehuetenango has been going well. To clarify, field-based training is designed to give trainees a taste of the situations they will encounter at their sites. This week we are in a village outside of Huehuetenango; we must be at least six or seven hours from Guatemala City by car. We are sleeping in a poorly insulated shack that was probably built in the 1960s. Everyone has to scrape copious amounts of rat feces off the bed before lying down. The entire "house" reeks of mold.

During the day, we build a ten-thousand-liter ferro-cement tank at a school. We also construct a much smaller tank at a household. We get back to the cabin at around five every day. Most of our free time is spent reading, listening to music, or just talking.

On a couple nights, we make a fire and roast marshmallows. It is frigid in Huehuetenango; if I had any say in the matter, I wouldn't choose to live in this department.

Site assignments will be handed out on Thursday, and everybody is pretty anxious. We have been working in this country for nearly two months with no idea of where each of us will be spending the next two years. Rumors have already started to fly. I just try to ignore them.

I get my first care package today from my parents—meaning that my mom sent me a bunch of fun stuff. The contents bring me ineffable joy: books, magazines, granola bars, and an effusively written card from my parents. I happily peruse a copy of the *Economist* and then realize that Peace Corps training is a quirky amalgam of summer camp, study abroad, and pledgeship. I will be a real Peace Corps volunteer in less than a month. I am ready.

JUNE 27, 2006

Unfortunately, one of my front teeth is starting to bother me. I hope it is nothing serious, even though that's unlikely. I am going to see a dentist in Guatemala City this morning. I am hurting. I am really hurting.

I get into Guatemala City, more commonly referred to as "Guate," and end up sharing a waiting room with several well-dressed ladinos (Guatemalans of European and Native American ancestry). The ladinos are the ethnic minority in the country. Generally speaking, they are far wealthier and better educated than the indigenous people. Ladinos wear Western clothing and speak Spanish as a first language. Usually they are taller and have lighter skin than indigenous Guatemalans.

Approximately two thirds of all Guatemalans are indigenous, though many polls show that far fewer Guatemalans identify themselves as indigenous. This could be because, in many ways, indigenous people are viewed as second-class citizens in Guatemala. Having been oppressed and manipulated for centuries, they wield little political and economic power compared to the ladinos.

Everyone in the waiting room is well-dressed … except for me. I am wearing a T-shirt and Levis, my unofficial Peace Corps uniform. Many people in the waiting room are reading *El Periódico,* the newspaper for the elite. In fact, *El Periódico* is probably the best news source in the entire country. This makes me feel a little better, even though the pain in my mouth has become excruciating. Shortly thereafter, I am told that I will need a root canal. Tomorrow will be a long day.

JUNE 28, 2006

My host mom and I have the same trivial conversation at dinner every night. If I don't consume at least six to eight beers before coming home, I am likely to die from boredom at the conclusion of every meal. We discuss the weather, our daily activities, and what we will do the following day. It's just me and her at the table. The rest of the family eats later. Really, the situation has become unbearably boring. But today is different. Today my host mom asks me if there's plenty of work in the United States. I tell her there is. She asks me if salaries are higher than in Guatemala. I tell her they are. She asks me why I joined the Peace Corps. I tell her it's complicated. There are many reasons. Mainly, I want to help someone besides myself. She thinks about that. I tell her the *huevos rancheros* are good and then grab one more tortilla to wipe my plate clean. I think that she has another question. I ask her to speak up if she has something on her mind. She asks me why some countries are so rich while others are so poor. She asks me if I think that is fair. She asks me if I think poverty will ever go away. I need to be careful with my answer. I tell her that I am not a very religious person, though I do believe in God. I tell her that I am not convinced that poverty is part of God's plan. I tell her that the world is a big place with hundreds of millions of people. I tell her that I suppose God is quite busy right now. And I tell her that God is not the only one with power; people can also accomplish something.

"Gracias, la cena estuvo bien."

"Buen provecho, Taylor.

Buen provecho is another strange Guatemalan idiom. It basically means "bon appétit," but the saying is used in a different way. A person who has finished eating says *gracias,* explicitly marking the conclusion of their meal. Immediately after that, one person or a group of people will say *buen provecho* in response.

The other possible scenario where *buen provecho* would be used: When a person is eating, at a restaurant for example, if another person enters or passes by that person already eating, then the passerby will say *buen provecho*. To this the appropriate response would be *gracias*. This makes little sense to me, but I am trying to adhere to cultural norms as best I can.

Site assignment is tomorrow afternoon. I'm not nearly as worried as some people. At the start of the application process, the Peace Corps does not even guarantee that the applicant, if accepted, will get his or her region of choice. What good would it do to worry about my site?

JUNE 30, 2006

The big day has finally arrived, and I am about to burst with anxiety. Upon entering the training center, I sense the tension. The anxiety is palpable; everybody will rest a little easier this afternoon. I wait to get called. I am brought into one of the training rooms. I'm told that I will be living in Nebaj in a department called El Quiché. Again, a department is the Guatemalan equivalent of an American state, and there are twenty-two departments in Guatemala. I'm excited. My heart is racing. I will be specializing in gravity-flow water systems. Later on, I fortuitously run into Kelsi Black at the training center. She's been in country for over a year and lives in Xexucap, just west of Nebaj. She seems cool. She's also the most attractive American I have seen down here.

In Nebaj, I will be working with Lynn Roberts, one of my Peace Corps trainers, and a nongovernmental organization (NGO) called Agua Para la Salud. Lynn actually founded the NGO fifteen years ago, which is impressive. Lynn is impressive. I've heard current Peace Corps volunteers compare him to MacGyver, the fictional television character who could solve myriad problems related to chemistry or engineering. From 1996 to 2006, Lynn Roberts was the Guatemala country coordinator for Water for People, a nonprofit international development organization based in Denver, Colorado. During that time, Water for People completed more than a hundred water, health, or sanitation projects in Guatemalan villages.

My principal duties within the NGO will include designing gravity-flow water systems, managing various development projects in the villages outside Nebaj, and grant writing. I am pumped. I cannot wait to leave the training center behind me.

Later on, our training group celebrates in Antigua. Formerly the capital of Guatemala, Antigua is now a tourist haven and a key hub for backpackers in Central America. I lose track of the time and miss the last taxi from Antigua back to Santo Tomás. I end up crashing with Kelsi, but before that we cavort from bar to bar, partying deep into the night. The lovely Kelsi and I share a double bed just off Antigua's central park at the Hotel Casa del Parque. Naturally, I have to make a concerted effort to keep my hands to myself. I succeed—primarily because I only have a few minutes of free time before I fall asleep.

JULY 1, 2006

From Antigua, I get on a camioneta headed for "Guate." I will get off at the *cruce*—an intersection between Santa Lucía Milpas Altas and Santo Tomás. I have a seat near the back and nearly puke from all the exhaust smoke. I have noticed that most of the camionetas used in Guatemala are from the state of Georgia. Basically, these are vehicles that are no longer legal to use in the United States. They are old, perhaps even outdated, and inherently more dangerous that what Americans are currently using. This doesn't bother me, though. It's obvious that I'm far more likely to get killed in an accident because of reckless driving; an old vehicle is the least of my worries.

I show up late for training today with a massive hangover. Luckily, it isn't raining. If it were, I would have arrived more disheveled than I already am. During the breaks over the course of the day, I try to avoid those in my group who are smokers. I'm still queasy, and a little cigarette smoke could have me vomiting in a hurry. Three other trainees slept in Antigua last night. Spending the night out, except during field-based training, is strictly prohibited for Peace Corps trainees, with rare exceptions. This is not good. Hopefully we won't get in trouble. This is the kind of mistake that gets people an early plane ticket back to the United States.

Early July 2006: Site Visits

Site visits usually occur during the third month of training. The trainees are given three to five days to actually visit their future town. It is a time to walk the streets, meet people, and hopefully find a place to live. Before traveling to Nebaj, the Appropriate Technology group will spend two days in Xela, Guatemala's second-largest city. We are there to officially meet our counterparts—the leaders of the organizations with whom we will be working for the next two years. Counterpart Day is traditionally an awkward and tedious experience, even more so for those volunteers who still don't speak much Spanish.

After some boring meetings, we wander around to explore. Xela, officially called Quetzaltenango, is a mesmerizing place. Unlike the capital, there is not that much violence in Xela. There's a major Guatemalan university here, and it's also a popular place for foreigners to study Spanish. Plus, there are a number of large volunteer organizations headquartered throughout the city. I also see several coffee shops and used bookstores. So far, I love the place. It appears to be a diverse, lively Guatemalan city with some subtle international flair.

Getting back to my job as a PCV, I will be working initially with Spanish engineer Daniel Pons. His mom is American and his dad is from Madrid, so he speaks both English and Spanish fluently. He has lived in Guatemala for about seven months. After speaking with him for five minutes, I know he's a cool guy. Now I am even more excited about moving to Nebaj.

July 11, 2006

Today, our training group votes to decide who will give a speech at the US ambassador's house during our swearing-in ceremony. None of us was even aware that a speech would be given at the ceremony. A few people are nominated, and votes are cast. Somehow, I have won in a landslide. This is pretty exciting. I will be the commencement speaker. Now I just have to think of something decent to say.

I finish my day the way I normally do, by reading in my poorly lit bedroom. *The Motorcycle Diaries* is a great travel journal. I don't have to like Guevara's politics to appreciate his writing. Interestingly, the journey that he and Alberto Granado took does not impress me. They only traveled for about half a year, and they never even left South America. I should stop ruminating; I need to work on my speech.

July 25, 2006

Today is the last official day of training. Our entire group eats lunch with US Ambassador James M. Derham at the training center. Derham, a career diplomat, was born in New York and studied mathematics in college. All the trainees were encouraged to bring thoughtful questions for him to answer. The entire session lasts about an hour. Ambassador Derham strikes me as a pragmatic and straightforward individual. I'm actually surprised that he wasn't more "diplomatic." After all, the man works in the diplomacy business. I think I enjoyed the lunch so much because he was candid with us. This is something one rarely sees when conversing with diplomats.

"How hard is it to support certain policies that you do not personally agree with? How do you deal with that?"

"That is a good question. And that is something that every person in my position deals with at some point during his career. Frankly, it's just part of the job."

"Mr. Ambassador, how do you go about convincing other countries to support your position on certain issues?"

"Well, that depends on what issue we're dealing with and with whom I'm speaking. Take the issue of Iraq as it relates to Guatemala. Who really cares what Guatemala thinks of Iraq? I say this because they don't have as much influence on United States foreign policy as other countries might. When necessary, if we are having trouble bringing a country to our side on an issue, we might use a little arm-twisting. Again, it really depends upon the specific issue being debated and with whom."

I have no doubt that Ambassador Derham is a Republican.

JULY 26, 2006

The big day has finally arrived. Today we swear in. I am only nervous because I have to speak. Last night I called my dad and read him my speech. My father is straightforward, a realist. So I felt pretty good when he described it as "outstanding."

At the ambassador's house, an odd mix of anxiety and joy fills the ceremony. All the guys are wearing ties. Most of the women are wearing nice dresses. I deliver my brief discourse behind an official US embassy podium. I speak into a microphone. I am told that I impressed the crowd with what I think was a nice blend of humor and inspiration. Thankfully, nobody knew how nervous I was. I shared the following words with my fellow trainees, the Peace Corps Guatemala administration, and a few embassy staffers and language teachers that morning:

"I would like to preface this by saying that when I went in to talk to Craig about what kind of speech this was supposed to be, he told me that it was like a commencement speech. I thought *okay, that makes sense,* but unfortunately—and this is just from my own experience—I hear the words 'commencement speech' and think two things: *long* and *boring.* So I will try to make this brief and even mildly entertaining, and then we can all head to Antigua for milkshakes.

"I want to begin by recognizing a few people. First, I would like to thank Ambassador Derham for allowing us to be sworn in under such luxurious circumstances. And Craig [the training director], I want you to know that I like your style. I want to thank all the Spanish teachers and everyone else at the training center; none of y'all's efforts go unnoticed. I also want to thank everyone in programming and administration from Peace Corps Guatemala and specifically my APCD, Basilio Estrada, because I know he gave me a really cool site. And I need to recognize all the folks at the medical office. I had to get a Guatemalan root canal a few weeks ago, and although I cannot describe the experience as a pleasurable one—in fact, I was terrified the entire time—I never once felt like I was getting anything but the best of care. Lastly, I want to give a very special thanks to my technical trainers, David Castillo and Lynn Roberts. When I came here, I knew nothing about working with cement. I had held a brick in my hand about six times in my life, and now I can build all kinds of cool technologies like stoves and rainwater catchment tanks. And I thank the other twenty-nine people in my training group. No one quit; I am proud of all y'all.

"So what can we say about training? Can we say that although training is entirely necessary, training is a sick and twisted version of summer camp mixed with study abroad, with even more rules than either of the two combined? If nothing else, every day was a gastrointestinal adventure—or perhaps the word *nightmare* is more appropriate.

"The most memorable moment of training for me was when we were out on the lawn at the training center in Santa Lucía and Craig made a comment about how we were all out here in Guatemala now, and that we were all kind of naked. I think Craig meant that maybe we're all feeling a little vulnerable, not knowing exactly what's going on, and that we were unsure of what to expect. I strongly agreed with the statement at the time.

But it's funny because, after being here three months, I still feel naked. I feel naked when I stand up here and say that the last three months haven't been easy for me, but there is nowhere else I would rather be. I have learned a lot about another language, culture, and people—both Guatemalans and Americans. Even more importantly, I have learned a lot about myself.

"We have chosen a life of meaning. If there is a more direct way to fight poverty, I would like to see it. A lot of people talk about fighting poverty with their money, and okay, that could work. Or you could fight it with your life by giving a part of yourself. You could come down to a place like Guatemala, eat the beans, ride the chicken buses, live in the villages, and try to change things!

"Before I left Texas, many people told me that two years was such a long time. I wondered how long those people were planning on living. People told me that the Peace Corps was a mistake. That it was risky and dangerous, that I was confused. Some people I know even said it was a mistake because I was not a hippie.

"So okay, if I could be serious for just a couple minutes, I would like to read a quotation. I like quotes, and I have been reading this one a lot lately. This one was written by a guy named James Allen. He said: 'Cherish your visions, cherish your ideals, cherish the music that stirs in your heart, the beauty that forms in your mind, the loveliness that drapes your purest thoughts, for out of them will grow all delightful conditions, all heavenly environment; of these, if you but remain true to them, your world will at last be built.'

"I think those words are highly relevant to why we are here today. I think Allen is telling us that it is okay to dream, and that we should never shy away from a challenge out of fear of failure or pain. I mean, most great accomplishments do not come easy.

"So barring some unforeseen medical breakthrough, in one hundred years we will all be dead. But if poverty still exists, the Peace Corps will still be here, as will the various reasons that brought us down to Guatemala: a desire to help others, to promote global understanding, or maybe some of y'all just came down here for the adventure of a lifetime. Right on! All of those reasons are still going to be around, because those reasons are timeless. We should never lose sight of that fact.

"Also, you hear a lot about the history of Peace Corps Guatemala during training. We are told about all of the tradition and success, and we have heard a certain number, the year 1963, several times. Yes, the Peace Corps has had a presence in Guatemala since 1963. Well, that is great, but that does not change the fact that a lot of the people we will be helping, especially kids, will be meeting Americans for the first time. We are the face of a nation, so when those poor kids think about America, they are going to think about fast food, Britney Spears, or some other terrible singers and movies where everybody gets blown up. But they will remember something even more clearly than all of that: the Peace Corps volunteer they got to know. They will remember the Peace Corps volunteer who lived in their hometown for two years. Really, we are the face of a nation abroad.

"It is an honor to be up here talking. It is an honor to represent America abroad. I cannot leave this podium today without saying that I love the United States, especially when I consider the caliber of people the US is capable of producing. So we're all going out to our sites soon, and it is not going to be anything like training, but who cares. We will finish what we started. I also think that is important to remember that y'all are all leaders. You should keep that in mind because, if nothing else, leadership is about sacrifice. Thank you."

After the official ceremony, everyone is snapping pictures and stuffing themselves with all kinds of finger foods. The ambassador lives in what appears to be a miniature country club. I wish I had brought a pitching wedge and a few balls. I had no idea a career diplomat could live amid such palatial surroundings. Switching gears, none of us has seen real cookies or decent finger foods for three months. We all sit around and stuff ourselves; everyone is so happy to have made it through training, largely because we have been told that training is the toughest part of the experience.

Later, we head to Assistant Country Director Jim Adriance's house for some *pupusas*, a Salvadoran food. Pupusas are made by stuffing maize-flour dough with at least one of the following—cheese, refried beans, pork rinds, beef—or a mix of those ingredients. They are cooked and then usually served with a cabbage relish. Pupusas are messy, unhealthy, and delicious. My forthcoming trip to El Salvador will revolve around pupusa-eating. Jim Adriance, like many Western diplomats and upper-level development workers, lives in a fabulous gated community in Zone 15. His house is also quite impressive; I love Spanish colonial architecture. Later on, we all head back to our host families. Tonight, everybody will be going out in Antigua, and I cannot wait.

JULY 27, 2006

I wake up in Antigua exhausted the following morning. This is a new feeling for me. Aside from the two field-based trainings, I only spent the night out on one or two other occasions. I have been following the Peace Corps Guatemala policy. Again, trainees are only allowed to spend one night away from their host families per month, excluding officially sanctioned Peace Corps Guatemala activities. When I did have to spend the night out, I had to sign a document at the Peace Corps training center giving them the name of the city I'd be visiting and the hostel where I'd be sleeping.

In Guatemala, all Peace Corps volunteers are entitled to two days away from their site per month. These days are not counted as vacation days. Days spent out of site for work or medical issues are not counted either. When a PCV is going to be out of his or her site for any reason, the PCV must call or e-mail Peace Corps Guatemala's safety and security coordinator. The PCV is expected to leave a clear and detailed message stating the dates he or she will be out of site, the location the PCV will be at, the nature of the visit, and any other relevant contact information. I wish this were a joke. It isn't. Peace Corps Guatemala is obsessed with knowing where all PCVs are at all times. Last night in Antigua, I was told that the Peace Corps had a specific reason for being so anal about safety and security policies.

Walt Poirier was last seen in La Paz, Bolivia, in 2001. He had been living in Bolivia as a Peace Corps volunteer for about six months. His disappearance prompted a congressional inquiry. In 2004, policymakers in Washington began to examine broader administrative and security issues within the Peace Corps—questioning whether Peace Corps officials were doing everything possible to keep PCVs safe. This is why the Peace Corps created an Office of Safety and Security in every country where Peace Corps has a presence, so that there's more supervision and oversight. Within each Peace Corps country, the Office of Safety and Security is run by an associate director. This person reports to the Peace Corps country director.

I would later find out that J. P. Gibbons, a guy from my training group, was friends with Walter Poirier at Notre Dame. J. P. would become a close friend over the next two years, but he didn't have much to say on the matter. What could he say?

I am back in Santo Tomás. The camioneta from Antigua took twenty minutes. I say hello to my host mom and tell her I need to pack. Lynn said he would drive me up to Nebaj after lunch. Lynn owns a house in Nebaj, but he also rents a small apartment in Antigua. He is always so busy. He frequently travels the country and gives PCVs advice on projects. Occasionally, he may even send an Agua Para la Salud mason to supervise a project in another Peace Corps Volunteer's site. Lynn also has to act as a tour guide when donors or prospective donors visit Guatemala. He will usually pick them up in Guatemala City and give a brief tour of Antigua. After couple of days of relaxation, he will drive with them to Nebaj or other sites so that people can look at some actual projects.

I realize I am lucky to have Lynn around; he is a tremendous resource and possesses a wealth of knowledge about the country. Lynn even said that I could rent a room in his house for my two years as a PCV. I am ecstatic. I didn't realize that that's where my colleague Daniel has been living.

We have been driving for about five hours. I have been enjoying the clear skies and good music. Lynn just threw in a Bob Marley cassette. I can't believe it. I used to have a poster of Bob Marley smoking a joint on my bedroom wall in Dallas. I listened to Marley more frequently as an adolescent, but I still love his music.

We just passed Sacapulas, a dry and hot town one hour south of Nebaj. This is it. My moment of truth has arrived. Forty-five minutes later, we begin our descent into Nebaj. It is located in the heart of the Ixil Triangle, an isolated region in northern Quiché. Chajul to the north and Cotzal to the east are the two other towns that form the triangle.

I look out my window awestruck. I have been assigned to live in an area of breathtaking natural beauty. I see an ocean of vibrant green before me. The mountains and hills gracefully surround the city center below. Even though it's nineteen hundred meters above sea level, Nebaj lies in a valley. Some of the surrounding villages are much higher up. I see thousands of trees and twelve shades of green. I see lonely pastures and fields of corn. I see horses and cows and farmers from afar. Then I see something else upon the horizon, though I can't be sure what it is. I see the immaculate beaches of Mexico and that gorgeous white sand. I see the streets of Buenos Aires, full of life, tango music, and beautiful women. I see Switzerland; I have a perfect view of the Alps from my window. I see the Italian Riviera; those quaint towns of Cinque Terra are so enjoyable in the summer. I see Berlin and then Munich. I see Prague and its unforgettable Gothic architecture. I see the rolling hills of Scotland, and I see Vienna. I see all of those friendly kids at the orphanage outside Quito. And I see the first bank I found in Montevideo. But then I see the Left Bank, and I remember the walk along the Seine River at night. I see the Paseo del Prado and the entrance to the Reina Sofia. I stroll through the Plaza Mayor, and I see the train station in Brussels. I see my dormitory in Innsbruck and the hotel I enjoyed in Amsterdam. I see all those journeys that have brought me to this point. I have seen so much. And I am thirsty for more.

I focus again on Nebaj. I was destined to come here. I will get to know this part of Guatemala quite well, better than I could have ever imagined. I have surprised myself; I am not scared. I would have been more anxious if I had known what I was getting into. Yet I did not. We pull into town. I stare out at Nebaj's huge central plaza. The place is teeming with people. The town's biggest church is enormous. Across the street, I see the municipal building, which doubles as the local police station. I see my new life and the opportunity of a lifetime.

"Taylor."

"Yeah, Lynn?"

"Welcome to Nebaj. Your new home."

We have arrived. And so it begins.

Four: Arrival in Nebaj

"I am still learning."

—*Michelangelo*

August 2006

I cannot complain about my living situation; it's much better than I could have ever imagined. Lynn's two-story house reminds me of an American ski lodge that was built in the 1980s. The lower level is made of cement, and the upper level is made mostly of wood. However, the second floor is still a work in progress. I see paint cans, brushes, and slabs of wood everywhere. Daniel and I each have our own bedroom. In the living room, we have a small television and a couple of plastic chairs. We also have a small refrigerator and some small wooden cabinets to store food. We even have a stove, though Daniel and I would mostly use the gas burners on top. In the downstairs bathroom, I see a decent toilet and an electric shower. The electric shower is a little scary, but I'm sure I'll get used to it. This is great. Four months ago, I figured I'd have to take bucket baths in my site.

Lynn lives in a small room upstairs, the only finished room on that level. The two parts of the house are entirely separate. I would soon discover that Lynn rarely spends any time downstairs. He is always considerate of my privacy and Daniel's.

I walk out onto the front porch and am amazed. Lynn has a beautiful garden and a nice, spacious backyard. I even see a hammock below, an ideal place to enjoy a novel or catch up on a few Peace Corps-issued copies of *Newsweek*. I return to my new bedroom to relax. Relieved yet still anxious, I sit at my desk and look around. I have inherited a wobbly wooden bookcase that is covered in mold. My desk is also wooden and equally moldy. I have a queen-size bed with sheets, though I would quickly realize that sheets provide insufficient protection against bugs. I would sleep in my sleeping bag for the next two years. My floor is dusty, but again I can't complain. During training, I was under the impression that I would be living in a wood shack or a tiny block "house" that differed only slightly from a prison cell. This is fantastic. I even have a small overhead light so that I can read at night. When sleeping in some of the smaller villages for work, my living conditions will be much more spartan—dirt floors, porous wooden walls, and farm animals running throughout the house.

THE JOB

For me and many other Peace Corps volunteers, there are two kinds of days: office days and field days. Office days—not surprisingly—entail large amounts of office work. For a water engineer, this could mean any number of assignments. During a more structured day in the office, I would hold a meeting or two with community leaders from the villages outside Nebaj. Here would be the time to plan a water survey or discuss budgetary issues and the parameters of work projects. All of the engineering work, like hydraulic design and mapmaking, is done at the office. Here I also prepare budgets and write project proposals for water projects. I am also responsible for translating documents for some of our American donors.

On the other hand, I also have field days. These field days are more like what people imagine when they think about a typical day in the life of an adventurous Peace Corps volunteer. The previously written sentence is already misleading, given the fact that a typical day does not exist. A field day would always include going out into one of the villages to do some type of work. Or I might just go in order to monitor an ongoing project. I could be gathering signatures for a work contract, though in reality I will almost always be gathering thumbprints since most illiterate people in Guatemala do not have signatures. Usually, I will be conducting a water survey with Diego Ramírez, the most experienced mason at Agua Para la Salud. I could also be conducting general health surveys at the school or from household to household. These field days can be the most challenging and, consequently, the most rewarding.

AUGUST 2006

Right now, I'm sitting under the eaves of a shack in Vicalamá, a hamlet two hours north of Nebaj by bus. It's amazing how quiet this place is compared to Nebaj. Nebaj is a town, not a city, but it's still a noisy place. I cannot ignore horns honking, people screaming, music blaring, or animals bleating throughout the day. And, for whatever reason, people always seem to be lighting loud fireworks in Nebaj, especially in the morning. But I hear none of that in Vicalamá; I only hear the unyielding rain.

I will sleep in this wooden shanty for the next four nights. We will be building some cement tanks to capture rainwater. The rain pours down incessantly this time of year. Now it's coming down really heavily—it sounds like our lamina roof might cave in. Heavy rain on lamina produces such a loud, deafening sound. It becomes harder to communicate; I have to speak up for the masons to hear me. We are waiting patiently for dinner. Our NGO has hired a cook for the week. This just means that we have paid a woman in town to cook food that we have purchased— mostly eggs, noodles, beans, and a variety of vegetables. We are on a tight budget. She will also bring several dozen corn tortillas for each meal. With all this rain, she'll be soaked by the time she makes it to our makeshift home.

I have yet to see a sewage system in this country. When it rains a lot, people just wallow in their own filth. It's quite disgusting. I still haven't learned to ignore all the trash and dog feces in the streets. Yet I am nonetheless astounded by the region's natural beauty. I have been blessed with the world's most beautiful cubicle. I am surrounded by verdant mountain ranges, the most stunning I have ever come across aside from those I saw in Switzerland. Far in the distance, I even see *milpas*—plots of maize for subsistence farming. I could not imagine tilling land on such a steep slope, but Ixils have mastered the art. Many might not even know what good plots of arable land look like. They may never have passed through Chimaltenango, where one sees huge nurseries and enormous plots of land. Those larger pieces of land in Chimaltenango are nearly flat, making them much easier to farm on.

The history of Guatemala is full of disparities, including land ownership. For the longest time, a small percentage of the ladino population has owned most of the land. The indigenous people have owned very little, and most of what they do own is less than ideal for farming. Who wants to plant crops at a forty-degree angle? This is one of the many sad stories in the country's history. Guatemala is a land of incredible natural beauty, countless natural resources, and an excellent climate for agriculture, but in many ways, it is a country stuck in time. It's a place where inertia tends to defeat progress, for now at least. Sadly, I discover that most Ixils I meet live only in the present. Based on my own observations, the classes held in the indigenous villages just look like perpetual snack breaks. I rarely hear the young people talk about what they want to be when they grow older. Nobody is thinking that far ahead. Their parents are trying to work hard today in order to put food on the table. In the Ixil Triangle, the future is tomorrow.

And so I begin to daydream. I've been in country over three months now. I'm still a novice, though I have learned a few things, some more important than others, about this benighted land. First, I've learned that Guatemala's nickname—"The land of eternal spring"—must have been coined by some clever members of the tourism industry. From what I've seen, there's nothing to be found in Ixil country that even vaguely resembles spring. On the other hand, Guatemala is an amazingly diverse country with several distinct climates. You can grow almost anything in the western highlands, including poppies. Maybe that is what people meant when they coined the term.

Secondly, I've learned that most rural Guatemalans are unable to grasp the concept of reading for pleasure. Every day after work this week, I've sat outside my shanty with a tattered paperback or a copy of the *Economist*. The community members view this as some sort of sadomasochistic gringo ritual.

"¿Buenas, por qué estás leyendo?"

"A mí me gusta leer mucho."

"¿Y no tiene dolor?"

"¿Cómo?"

"¿No tiene dolor de ojo?"

"Para nada."

"Usted se siente triste entonces."

"¡Como pudiera estar triste!"

"Pues gringo, hay muchas palabras, demasiadas. No nos gusta leer tanto."

"Hello, why are you reading?"

"I like to read a lot."

"And your eyes don't hurt?"

"No."

"Are you sad then?"

"Why would I be sad?!"

"Well gringo, there's a lot of words there, too many words. We don't like to read much."

To be fair, reading probably would not be nearly as enjoyable if I were illiterate, or if I could only read at an elementary level. However, reading is an essential component of my life here. I love to read. I passionately gobble up pages every day; my literary appetite never fades. Even more relevant is the fact that there's not much else to do out here. I think back to the last day of training. I was nervous about moving to my site, and understandably so. But I would have been infinitely more nervous if I didn't love to read.

I have also learned that indigenous Guatemalans refuse to walk unless they have to. As long as it's not raining, I normally leave our shack to explore after dinner. I always make sure to bring my poncho. Out here, I often feel like I'm walking around in a *National Geographic* magazine. As usual, people stare at me like I have gone mad. Because I'm American, the villagers think I'm rich. Since I'm rich, I don't need to walk because I could just pay someone to drive me around. I shouldn't be strolling anywhere. Yep. Walking for leisure is an abstruse concept in the indigenous villages of Guatemala.

I cannot help but notice the *traje* (female indigenous clothing) the women wear, because it is so beautiful. All of it is handmade and takes a great deal of time to make. In Nebaj, the *corte* (dress) is typically burgundy with thin stripes. It is made of thinner fabric than the others I have seen in Guatemala so far. It is also worn more snugly. The *huipiles* (blouses) in Nebaj are the most beautiful I have ever seen. They are normally made of greens, purples, and yellows. As part of the design, they feature intricate embroidery of humans and animals. Lynn told me that sophisticated geometric designs are also part of the huipiles, but I haven't yet noticed that. I've also seen women wearing some sort of headdress with fluffy pompoms and highly colorful ribbons. Many times, the outfits include a shawl as well. The shawl is like a backpack for Mayan women, but they also use it to carry their children. In indigenous communities, wearing the traditional dress is one of the most important aspects of the lifestyle. At times, I feel that I am living in the last untouched place on earth. These people have managed to preserve their time-honored ways.

AUGUST 2006

The Pleasure of My Company is hilarious. I do not want the story to end. Steve Martin is a genius. He writes with such elegance and wit. I wish I could do that, but I don't think I've got the gift. Some deep thinker probably said, "Many knock on the door of literary greatness, yet few enter its sanctuary." I don't know why I've been put on this planet. I hope that two years in Nebaj will shed some light on the matter. I know I'll have plenty of time to think.

AUGUST 3, 2006

Taking a break from work with Agua Para la Salud masons Antonio Cavinal and Pedro de Paz, I eat my lunch of rice, refried beans, and tortillas on top of a spring box that I helped build. The sun beats down on us all day. I keep reapplying sunscreen. The masons laughed at me when I brought that out for the first time, but I didn't care. I suppose I would laugh if I were in their position.

A spring box captures water directly from its source. Our NGO uses reinforced concrete to build them. The idea is to make all aspects of the water system strong enough to last for at least twenty years. With spring boxes, we also want to prevent contamination from outside sources. They usually take one to two weeks to build. Upon completion of the entire water system, the spring box and distribution tank will be locked, and the community's water committee will be given the keys. The villagers will be responsible for cleaning the spring box and the distribution tank every few months. Since the masons still don't know me well, the conversation invariably turns toward tortilla consumption.

"¿Pues Taylor, ¿qué piensas de la tortilla? ¿Está bien?"

"¡Cómo no!"

"Porque a veces hay voluntarios, y a ellos no les gustan. Había una chica de Francia y no podía comer nada de tortilla."

"Me gustan las tortillas. Solamente que no puedo comer cien por día como Ustedes."

Now everybody's laughing.

"Vaya, está bien pues. Comemos más entonces."

"Taylor, what do you think of tortillas? Do you like them?"

"Of course!"

"Because sometimes there are volunteers that don't like them. There was this one French girl who never ate tortillas."

"I like tortillas. I just can't eat one hundred a day like you guys."

"Okay, that's alright. Let's eat some more then."

The masons then confess to eating approximately twenty tortillas per day. The number would be higher, they tell me, if they could stomach more than four or five for breakfast. For me, that kind of tortilla consumption is inconceivable. These aren't even very tasty tortillas; they are dry and flavorless. These guys really are *hombres de maiz.*

I learned about the *Popul Vuh*, the Mayan's version of the Holy Bible, during training. It tells the creation story of the Mayans and was written in Quiché, one of the country's most widely spoken indigenous languages. It is widely held that the book was written sometime during the sixteenth century, even though the stories had been previously written in hieroglyphics hundreds of years before. The Mayans had lived well in southern Mexico and Guatemala for centuries, but the arrival of the Spaniards in the sixteenth century changed all that. The Spanish eventually gained control of the Yucatán Peninsula, persecuted the Mayans, and burned most of their books. Nevertheless, the Mayans continued to pass the tales on orally. Within the text, the story talks about God's attempt to create humans, asserting that God made men from maize instead of mud like it says in the Bible. Even today in the villages, maize is considered to be a sacred food. It is an integral part of village life. Already I have see many men refuse to begin eating if tortillas have not been served.

The indigenous people rely heavily on maize for survival, but this can lead to problems. A diet that consists mostly of corn, rice, and beans is not necessarily very balanced. Children's brains are not able to fully develop if they don't get to eat enough protein.

Furthermore, chronic malnutrition can lead to all kinds of birth defects, many of which could probably be prevented by taking a multivitamin daily.

AUGUST 4, 2006

Friday has arrived; everyone is eager to return to Nebaj. I am tired. I haven't slept well all week. I'm ready for a shower. After five days, things get a bit unsanitary in the mountains. Come to think of it, I haven't seen either of the masons brush their teeth this week.

The two-hour ride back on the camioneta is a gorgeous one. In spite of all the foul odors, everyone seems to be enjoying the best of Latin American pop music. So far we have heard Maná, Ricardo Arjona, and Juanes. I enter my house exhausted and filthy. I have been yearning for a shower since Monday evening, yet I choose not to take one that night. I am just too tired. Hygiene is secondary in the Peace Corps. Any PCV who says otherwise is kidding himself. Mental health is what matters most.

Lying on my bed, I consider my current state of affairs. I think about how long I'll be living here. Essentially, I signed twenty-seven months of my life away to the Peace Corps and the United States government. Two years of my mid-twenties will be gone. Will this experience break me? Will I pick up some lethal parasite or get caught in the middle of gang-related violence? Or will I die when the Quiché-Guate camioneta rounds a corner a little too sharply, falls off the side of a cliff, and kills most passengers in the process? Have I come here to die? Or will I leave stronger, more confident? I'm not bitter, just a little confused. These paroxysms of doubt don't make me weak, only human, or so I hope. I don't pretend to have it all figured out; I still hope this odyssey will clarify some of my lingering apprehensions. Is this merely wishful thinking?

AUGUST 10, 2006

Having recovered from a week in the mountains with the masons, I go over water-system design with Daniel at the office in Nebaj today. Daniel is supposed to teach me the basics of hydraulic engineering, of which I know nothing. Daniel will move back to Madrid next month to pursue a master's degree in engineering. He has been scatterbrained at the office recently, which isn't helpful. After work, we go to El Descanso for dinner and a few beers.

El Descanso is an essential element of life in Nebaj for most development workers and tourists. This two-story restaurant-bar combination was founded by a couple of PCVs in 2001 as a sustainable development project, but has been locally owned for the past three years. El Descanso has several computers with Internet access. The key to this spot lies in its restaurant-bar area. Because of the foreign influence, they play great music, everything from Radiohead to Otis Redding. Drinking here is a great way to forget about the reality of living and working in Nebaj. Both levels remind me of a standard low-budget hostel in Western Europe. And the balcony provides a panoramic view of Nebaj and its environs. They also run hiking tours out of the place, which isn't really necessary. Hiking around Nebaj is perfectly safe, and the trails are easy to follow. Hiring a guide might be useful in the Amazon or the Vatican Museum, but not here.

While living in Nebaj, it is vital to introduce oneself to all the employees at El Descanso as soon as possible. These are all young Ixils who can become good friends. Surprisingly, there isn't much turnover at this place. Besides, they can save a starving volunteer a few quetzales from time to time, in the form of free booze or free time on the Internet. Either way, it's a good deal.

That evening, we meet some volunteers for Observers of the Peace. I have never heard of this organization, and I quickly realize why. They don't do a whole lot with regard to work. It sounds like they just go out for ice cream, drink boxed wine, and complain about American foreign policy. I am able to confirm that the bulk of their work in Guatemala does involve "observing."

AUGUST 2006

I spend my Saturday morning finishing *The Horse Whisperer.* Six months ago, I would not have been confident enough to formulate this sentence even if it were true. This is a girly book, and I've already seen the movie, so reading the book now makes even less sense. But at least I am trying something that I would not ordinarily read. This is pure escapism. I learn nothing from the book.

Before coming to Guatemala, I was worried that there would be a shortage of good books available in English. My concerns were unfounded. I have access to a couple hundred books in Nebaj alone, mainly because of Lynn's personal collection at his house. Besides, the book culture in the Peace Corps is nothing short of inspiring. My fellow volunteers are always talking about books, sharing favorites, comparing writing styles, and denouncing authors or genres. It's great to be around such well-read and opinionated people.

The Nebaj market on Sundays is an enormous mess. The streets are teeming with people, many of whom have traveled two to three hours or more to sell their goods—mostly fruits and vegetables. But many other items are sold there: popcorn, flour, salt, sugar, ginger, noodles, tomato sauce, toys, pirated DVDs, T-shirts, flowers, soap, scissors, razors, shampoo, bags, coffee, tea. The market has it all. I am learning how to bargain with the indigenous women. I have to be tough with these little ladies. I am a new guy in town. Nobody recognizes me yet. That will change.

Huge portions of the place reek of human waste. Market day in Nebaj falls on Thursday and Sunday. Years ago, these were the only market days. However, the population in the Ixil Triangle has exploded in the last twenty years. So I can take advantage of a smaller market on the other days. This makes my life much easier. In many Guatemalan villages, there is only one day to buy food. But since Nebaj has a market every day, I am not compelled to buy all my food for the week on Sundays. The chaotic scene on Sundays is compounded exponentially by the many alcoholics stumbling around town. Sunday is the day of the drunks in Guatemala, a country rife with alcoholism. Usually on Sundays, I will see several men passed out in the street, often in the morning. Others will wander around town screaming in Ixil or crying. Sure, there are alcoholics in the United States, too. But I've yet to witness a grown man pass out in the street. Things are just different down here.

I decide to try Comedor Lupita for lunch. Located just east of Nebaj's main square, this *comedor* would become a second home. I had no idea that I would eat there at least a hundred times over the course of the next two years.

Not surprisingly, a middle-aged woman, Lupita, runs the show. She speaks excellent Spanish, a huge plus in Nebaj, and she is quite friendly. For only fifteen quetzales, I am given a huge portion of yellow rice, a small salad, a main dish like grilled beef or fried chicken, and as many tortillas as I can handle. I usually drink *agua pura*. The food is excellent. I leave stuffed. I probably added too much *picante*, homemade hot sauce, to my meal. I finished my meal less than five minutes ago, and the heartburn has arrived. I thank Lupita, pay her, and rush home to eat some antacids. Chronic heartburn, which would eventually become acid reflux, would be my primary health concern during my time in Guatemala.

AUGUST 20, 2006: PEACE CORPS WELCOMING PARTY IN PACHALUM

Welcoming parties are an institution in Peace Corps Guatemala. For lack of anything else to celebrate, each department routinely welcomes new volunteers every three months. These nights usually revolve around an abundance of cheap alcohol, good fun, and immature drinking games. In college, my friends and I never needed any positive motivational influence to consume alcohol. On the other hand, it appears that most PCVs in Guatemala are very excited about them. Because of my obvious lack of enthusiasm for drinking games, I am quickly denounced as an outsider. But I do pay attention and learn a few things. I sorely miss my drinking buddies from college; a few of the PCVs I meet are so zealously idealistic they come across as immature and naive. For example, I was even criticized for purchasing Styrofoam cups because they "put holes in our ozone." As if there were innumerable environmentally conscious options at the *tienda* across the street from Stacy's house. I was under the illusion that a Styrofoam cup would be a relatively benign way to get the rum into my body. I am not an environmentalist, nor am I a bad person.

Five: Water Engineering

"To live without hope is to cease to live."
—*Fyodor Dostoyevsky*

Back in Nebaj, I continue to study hydraulics with Daniel. He'll be leaving soon, so I need to be prepared to do all the water engineering at Agua Para la Salud. Designing water systems is not as fancy as it sounds. Anyone with a high-school education could probably do it. The most difficult part is manipulating a few formulas, fairly straightforward math. But this is not a classroom—this is real life. If I get a "B" on a water project, I may have wasted thousands of dollars. Or worse, the system may not last as long as it's supposed to. The people I am trying to help have seen enough hardship. I need to focus and do things right.

In a few minutes, we'll travel to a town called Jacaná for a topographical survey. This will be my last one with Daniel. After that, it'll just be me and Diego. At this point, I am overwhelmed and nervous. In less than a month, I will be the only water engineer working at the NGO. What if I fail? What if I don't manipulate the equations on the spreadsheet properly? What if I show poor leadership in the field during one of the surveys? If something goes wrong out there, I will have no one to blame but myself. The Peace Corps is quickly becoming a lesson in accountability.

The survey in Jacaná lasts only three days. We take measurements with our yellow measuring tape. Diego measures the change in altitude with the Abney level, a hand level used to find elevations and angles. I check the orientation with the compass. We record all this information and take notes on our surroundings whenever necessary. Villagers help by guiding us through the rugged terrain and clearing brush whenever necessary. One of them also holds a stick that we have marked at Diego's eye level prior to starting the survey. This way we can figure out the change in altitude, if there is any. Today is tough; the rain starts early and does not let up. I am the one with the clipboard. Recording all the information is a nightmare. I try to cover the clipboard with my poncho, but don't have much success. The ink smears on all the pages, but at least I can still read my own writing. Doing a water survey in the rain is no fun.

For this particular survey, we need to use galvanized iron tubes in a few places instead of standard PVC, since the tubing will be left exposed—when the distribution line crosses a river, for example. Using a small amount of galvanized pipe is common. We try to use as little as possible, because those tubes are at least four or five times more expensive than PVC pipe.

We mark the potential site for the distribution tank. We number all the houses; each family working on the project will get a *chorro* (spigot) to their house. We do all this, and on Wednesday afternoon, we return to Nebaj. Tomorrow I need to put all the survey information into a Microsoft Excel spreadsheet, manipulate some formulas, confer with Diego, and design the water system. After a long shower at my house, I take my laundry up to Popi's, also known as Don's.

Popi's Restaurant and Hostel is owned and run by American Don Langley. The man is one of the craziest, most remarkable characters I have ever met. Don moved to Nebaj in 2002, but has lived in Central America for the last twenty-five years. He was once a US Marine, and there are rumors that he worked for the National Security Agency in Southeast Asia in the late 1960s.

I've never seen him drink, though he huffs about four packs of cigarettes per day. He looks like a present-day NFL defensive lineman except for his massive gut. He's sometimes a rude and finicky man, though he's an outstanding conversationalist when he wants to be. This big guy has a big heart. Don runs a charity of the standard 501(c)(3) variety called Mayan Hope. For the past four years in Ixil country, Mayan Hope has focused on funding education for young people who otherwise would not be able to afford it.

As I enter the restaurant-*cum*-hostel, I catch a glorious whiff of banana bread. Don must be baking a few loaves. Then a flicker of shame rises up in me. My clothes are disgusting. The little indigenous ladies working here must think I'm an animal, that I live in a pigsty and have no self-respect. I need to face reality. I live in rural Guatemala. I boil water every day to kill disease-inducing organisms. I eat thirty or forty bananas a week. I haven't had a decent bowel movement since I moved to Nebaj. I walk everywhere. I read voraciously. I put all my toilet paper in a garbage can because the pipes can't handle toilet paper. I burn trash. I go to bed early; I go to bed earlier than my grandmother. And I wake up early. I live in my Levis. I shower only twice a week because anything more would be excessive. I live and work in the middle of nowhere. I roll around in the mud with indigenous people when I conduct these water surveys. After that, I take my nasty clothes to Popi's. This is Peace Corps. I miss my friends and family. I miss Texas just like I miss Buenos Aires, Spain, and Innsbruck. I especially miss Innsbruck. I miss the view from my dorm room. I miss the conversations my buddy Alex and I had, drinking cheap red wine out of tiny glasses. Back then, we used to pick red wines for under three Euros a bottle based solely on the look of their labels. I miss the smell of Europe, great beer, and going to class in the Swiss Alps. At the University of Innsbruck, I took two classes taught by Dr. Loch Johnson—the best teacher I've ever had. I miss him so much. But this is the life I wanted, and so there can be no complaining.

SEPTEMBER 2006: DANIEL'S DESPEDIDA

Tonight is Daniel's last night in Nebaj. This means that we'll be eating a nice meal at a comedor with all the guys from work. A *comedor* is Guatemala's version of an inexpensive café. Many times, comedores are merely extensions of people's houses. Comedores serve simple Guatemalan food. To survive in this country on a meager Peace Corps stipend, comedores are essential. In Nebaj, I can get an excellent meal at one of these places for thirteen to twenty quetzales, whereas a trip to McDonald's or Wendy's in the capital would cost me at least three times that amount.

After dinner we will head to Three Two One, Nebaj's one and only whorehouse masquerading as a strip club. The masons, being small and indigenous, cannot drink all that much. However, they do drink quickly. I have never been to Three Two One, so I'm kind of excited as we walk over there from the cantina. I am also embarrassed, but I think my shame will subside with more beer. I have only been to a strip club on one other occasion, and that was as a college student in Athens. I disliked the entire experience. I felt dirty for weeks after that. For me, this will be more of a sociological study than a chance to see naked women. I have been told that the women there are not very attractive. I would find out that this is a gross understatement.

Immediately after entering this shady establishment, I feel like a dirty old man. The place is disgusting. Most of the men are too drunk to speak coherently. I see empty bottles of *aguardiente* everywhere. *Aguardiente*, literally translated to mean "firewater," is cheap, sugarcane-based liquor. This is the liquor of choice in Guatemala's indigenous villages. It's usually much cheaper than clear rum. The stuff is absolutely disgusting; merely smelling an empty bottle makes me a bit queasy.

The two women dancing on the makeshift stage are overweight and homely. At least they have a pole to work with; I was not even expecting that level of sophistication. The evening will not end soon enough. I pound beer after beer to desensitize myself.

Finally, at three in the morning, we stumble out of there and walk home.

SEPTEMBER 2006

Diego and I are off to do another water survey in Kalompatzom, a village about forty minutes outside of Nebaj by car. We arrive there and discover that the spring site—where we would normally start the survey—is a three-hour walk from the town. We are in for a grueling day, the quintessential Peace Corps day. We must negotiate difficult terrain for three hours. Only after that will we begin our survey. For lunch, the community members gave Diego and me one hard-boiled egg and a stack of hot tortillas with a container of chili sauce. Naturally, most of the lunch conversation is in Ixil, of which I know only a few words. I space out and enjoy my lunch.

I get back to my house in Nebaj only to discover that my shoes are soaked. How had I not noticed this earlier? I have serious work to do for the rest of the week, and I need these shoes to be dry. I will head back to the village tomorrow morning, so I need to dry these shoes in a hurry. I decide to remedy the problem by placing my shoes in the oven. This will be a quick bake. They're significantly drier after about thirty minutes in the oven. I think pre-heating made the difference.

SEPTEMBER 9, 2006

It's four in the morning. My University of Georgia Bulldogs are playing the South Carolina Gamecocks today. I want to see this football game. I need to see this football game. If I am a man, I must prove it by watching this game of tackle football. This can only be done in Guatemala City or Antigua. I remind myself that Hemingway described courage as "grace under pressure." I decide to travel to Antigua for one night. Yes, I will face twelve to fifteen hours of travel just to spend one night in that lovely colonial town and watch my beloved Dawgs mix it up with Steve

Spurrier's Gamecocks. I board a camioneta at 5:00 a.m. I cannot believe this is happening.

I am at Mono Loco by 11:40 a.m., over an hour before kickoff. This sports bar is one of the most popular spots in town—both with locals and tourists. More importantly, it's one of only two places to watch college football in Antigua on Saturdays. The other bar is called Red's, located near the famous Santa Catalina Arch. The beautiful thing about the Mono Loco is that Peace Corps volunteers get a special discount on drinks. For every liquor drink we order, we are given a double for the price of a single. Compared to the cost of living in a volunteer's site, Antigua is an extremely expensive place to visit. Thus, this drink special is not taken lightly. Mono Loco serves overpriced American-style food, which I can't afford, so I usually eat elsewhere.

UGA dominates on both sides of the ball and cruises to an 18-0 win. I can't feel too satisfied; it's too early in the season for that.

MID-SEPTEMBER 2006

My weekend is over. Diego and I travel to Kalompatzom to continue our water survey. I can't help but notice the squishy sounds our feet make as we climb up the mountain on our way to the spring site. It rained hard last night. The villagers stare at me as if I am working for NASA. They are literally awestruck by my every move. One of them touches my clipboard and says I'm a lot like current president Oscar Berger. Wow. One of the men asks me what I eat for breakfast in the United States. I tell him I occasionally eat eggs, and he asks if I'm joking. Yes sir, we have eggs in the United States. Another tells me he thinks the sun is currently overpopulated. I prudently decide it would be unwise to contradict him since I have just arrived in town. He then asks me if there are rivers in the United States. I tell him that not only are there rivers, but that we also have trees. I may have said too much, because I heard a lot of frantic talking in Ixil after that. My goal is not to belittle these people. But some of life's experiences should never be forgotten. Illiteracy is such a destructive force, yet education is a gift that most of my countrymen take for granted. I wish I could do more to raise awareness. I wish that inequalities in Guatemala were not so extreme. I will never understand how a benevolent God can allow this to happen. It just isn't fair.

Whoever said that poverty is a virtue has never traveled to Guatemala's western highlands. Poverty is misery. Poverty is sadness. Poverty is relentless oppression. Poverty is destruction. Poverty kills until enough people rise up in anger to defeat it. Just because the eradication of poverty may take centuries to accomplish doesn't mean it shouldn't be handled with urgency. This is a cause worth fighting for. I agree with microfinance pioneer and Nobel Prize-winner Muhammad Yunus: one day, poverty will be history, merely one more thing to observe in a museum. I hope I'm still alive to see it, even though I'm not too optimistic about that.

MID-SEPTEMBER 2006: ANTS IN MY PANTS

After four days, Diego and I have still not finished the water survey in Kalompatzom. Hopefully today, Friday, will be the last day. These men were so impressed with my sagacity yesterday, but that can change quickly. I am especially tired this morning, and I do not know why. After we have walked for at least a kilometer or two, I suddenly realize that I must have unwittingly stepped in one of the Ixil Triangle's innumerable anthills. My problems that morning have just begun. My legs and feet are covered with ants. They all seem to be biting me in concert. I frantically drop the clipboard and Abney level, trying to stave off these tiny monsters. After an intense ten-minute battle, I think I have gotten most of them off of my juicy skin. Only then do I realize that I have been putting on quite a show. About ten of the community members, all of whom had been helping clear brush for the survey, were on the ground laughing at me. This continued for another ten or fifteen minutes. I cannot remember ever feeling so embarrassed. I am supposed to be a community leader and bring water to various villages, yet I can't even manage to avoid an anthill. Between my two legs and ankles, I am probably staring at eighty to one hundred bites. I am feeling a little nonplussed and not just because of the shame factor. I have never been eaten up by ants like this before. Here I am in the middle of nowhere, surrounded by indigenous men who hardly even speak Spanish. What will I do if I have an allergic reaction? I decide to call Lynn, hoping he will shower me with some of his limitless wisdom. After hurriedly explaining the situation to him, the following exchange ensues:

"Well, how are you feeling right now, Taylor?"

"Fine, I guess."

"Are you having trouble breathing?"

"No, well, I mean, I don't think so. Should I be having trouble breathing?"

"Well, Taylor, I think you're probably fine. Take a Benadryl or any antihistamine if you have one in your bag. And if you start feeling funny, get your ass back to Nebaj, because you could be having some type of allergic reaction. We just don't want you to go into anaphylactic shock. You hear me?"

"Right, Lynn, thanks. I'll see you back at the house tonight."

"Okay, Taylor, take care."

We finish our survey that afternoon. I eat a late lunch at the home of Francisco, the village president. This is quite an honor. I would have assumed that Francisco is one of the wealthiest men in town, yet his wooden house looks like everyone else's. Chickens, rabbits, and dirty cats are wandering all over the dirt floors. His wife uses a brick stove for cooking, instead of just piling up sticks on the ground. I see a small wooden table out of the corner of my eye. I see one large bed. Francisco has told me that he has a large family, so I am not sure what their sleeping arrangements are. Maybe they use cots that they put away during the day.

We enjoy the Ixil specialty *boxbol* with a steaming mound of tamales. Boxbol is traditional food in the Ixil Triangle. It's basically just corn dough wrapped in leaves that have been boiled or cooked over a fire. It is usually eaten with a homemade hot sauce. Boxbol is surprisingly tasty. However, I could only eat it every once in a while.

OCTOBER 3, 2006: PEACE CORPS NEPAL IN THE 1970S

I arrive at the office for a busy day of Microsoft Excel spreadsheets and formulas. John is currently renting out an extra room at the Agua Para la Salud office. He also happens to be the interim country director for Water for People. John was hired as country coordinator after Lynn resigned in 2006. I will willfully omit John's last name. I don't know how to spell it anyway.

And so right now, John is smoking a joint in the courtyard. It's nine in the morning! At our office! As country director, John has a lot fiscal power, but he doesn't seem to give a damn about anything. He's so honest. He's too honest—like he shoots some sort of government-issued truth serum into his veins every morning. I admit I do like having the guy around. There's nothing more entertaining than hearing John recount his own experiences as a Peace Corps volunteer in Nepal in the 1970s.

"What do you really think of the Peace Corps, Taylor?"

"I don't know, John. I like it all right so far, but I've been in country for less than six months."

"I wonder how much has changed since the 1970s. It was absolute chaos in Nepal in the 1970s. I did some work, designed a few water systems, but I don't think the Peace Corps administration back in the capital really cared. You know I never got one piece of mail from them or anyone else during those two years?"

"Really, John? That seems odd."

"Yeah, Taylor, you know what I think? I don't even think they knew exactly where I was living. I was never asked for my official address. I never even had anyone come visit my site."

"That does sound strange. The Peace Corps probably has changed a lot since your days in Nepal. Right now, the Peace Corps administrators in Guatemala seem more concerned with pleasing those bureaucrats in DC at any cost. Sometimes I feel like the Peace Corps is more of a public-relations campaign than anything else."

"I know, Taylor. You've got to make sure you're in this for the right reasons. A lot of people are in development for the wrong reasons. You just wait; you'll see what I'm talking about."

John was right. Eventually I would see what he was talking about.

OCTOBER 7, 2006: SATURDAY AT EL DESCANSO

Several development workers are relaxing at El Descanso. All of us are working on ice-cold bottles of Gallo. Those present include a lawyer from Barcelona named Dani; Basques Javier and Mikel, who are working in local schools; fellow PCV Jeff Reckner; an Ixil named Otto who works as a painter; a Belgian named Eric who works in a honey cooperative; and me. Some lively debates have taken place here, but it depends on the crowd. Mikel has struck up a conversation comparing Spanish and French nationalism. I am having a little trouble hearing everyone on account of the rain. There must be a leak in the roof; small drops of rain are landing on our table.

"Francia es mucho más nacionalista que España."

"¿Pero estás seguro de eso?"

"¿Y eso … ya eres de Francia ahora?"

"Es una pregunta amigo, solo eso."

"¿Bueno, tiene algo que ver con la historia de los dos países no? Y sobre todo el fascismo."

"Vale, de acuerdo, pare mí es mucho mas importante ser vasco que ser español."

"¿Y que pensáis vosostros?"

"France is much more nationalist than Spain."

"But are you sure about that?"

"What you're French now?"

"It's just a question, buddy, nothing more."

"Well, it has something to do with the history of the two countries and, especially, fascism."

"Okay, I agree. For me it's much more important to be Basque than to be Spanish."

"What do you all think?"

I know better than to comment here. I am opinionated, but I am still feeling like the newbie in town. For now, I'm happy to enjoy my beer and let the Europeans question the merits of various ideological positions in Europe.

OCTOBER 2006

I show a potential donor—Ted Kuepper from Global Water, a Los Angeles-based NGO—around town with Lynn. Because of Lynn, Global Water is interested in working with Agua Para la Salud. I would have never guessed that Mr. Kuepper was in the Navy for twenty years. He is scared to death of the food in Nebaj. He eats PowerBars almost exclusively for four consecutive days. At least Lynn takes him to Don's a couple times.

OCTOBER 13-14, 2006

A large group of PCVs spend the weekend in Antigua for some rest and relaxation. Most of us are sleeping at 58B.

The 58B, creatively titled for its street address, was the first de facto hostel of Peace Corps Guatemala. PCVs have been crashing here for decades. Also called just "The B," this place is essentially a big house situated near the Antigua bus terminal. In fact, a large Antiguan family still lives here. They offer about fifteen modest rooms at a cheap rate. A single goes for 30Q and a double costs 50Q.

The 58B is bereft of North American amenities. The showers are cold. The rooms are drab and bare. The walls are paper-thin, therefore there's little or no privacy. Yet the place is good enough for many PCVs—especially since most folks just need somewhere to pass out after a night of heavy boozing. Most people forget about those paper-thin walls. This can make for some interesting nights and conspicuous sexual encounters. Some of these encounters will result in unforgettably awkward mornings afterward. Tonight is one of those nights. The noisy couple is on the first floor, but they are so loud, they might as well be sharing a bed with me. I'm just glad it's not me down there. Those two will regret it tomorrow morning.

OCTOBER 18, 2006

Today is a sad day, especially for members of my training group. We have lost someone for the first time: superstar volunteer B. J. Osorio has been medically separated. B. J. separated his shoulder while going for a jog in his site in Huehuetenango. I remember him telling me during training that he had hurt his right shoulder several times before. I had also heard that at certain times PCVs will feel like they are swimming in an ocean of government-mandated red tape. Now I have seen it firsthand.

Peace Corps Washington coldly enforces those rules and regulations that many volunteers come to detest. I understand that some rules are necessary, but some medical cases should be considered on an individual basis. To be brief, B. J. separated his shoulder, and his rehabilitation was going to last for more than three months. In the minds of those Peace Corps paper pushers in DC, his situation is untenable because no PCV is allowed to take a leave of absence for more than ninety days because of an injury. I give B. J. a call that day just to wish him luck.

"How are you holding up, fella?"

"I mean, what can I say? This sucks. I deferred UGA law school to come down here. It took me like a year to apply. Now I'm going home."

"I know it, man. I'm sorry."

"It just sucks because now I'm going to have to make a lot of decisions that I really, really don't want to make right now."

"Well, shoot me an e-mail after you get settled."

"All right, I'll probably call you after Georgia-Florida, especially if we win."

"That sounds good, B. J."

He's down, but I know he will get over it. I hang up the phone with him and am left fixated upon one thing: the Peace Corps is an ephemeral experience. I think I am tough enough, and I don't plan on quitting, but what if something unforeseen happens? If I am forced to leave like B.J., I will board the plane with a bitter taste in my mouth. I will keep my head up, though—at least I tried.

OCTOBER 26, 2006

The masons I work with at Agua Para la Salud are poor and incredibly frugal. I have been working with them for three months and have yet to see them spend money on anything except a few beers at the end of the week. Coming to Guatemala, I have a clearer understanding of how cumbersome, how utterly suffocating parenthood can be for the destitute. And this assessment doesn't reflect the emotional element involved. All of the six masons have at least a couple of children, but most of them have four or five. The guys are paid the equivalent of about four hundred dollars a month—not a bad salary by Guatemalan standards. A day laborer in Guatemala typically earns between seven and eight US dollars a day; most of the APS masons are making over twice that amount. I know all this because I write the project proposals at our office, which include financial statements and budgets. Four hundred dollars per month—that is almost exactly the same as my Peace Corps stipend. But I also have health and dental insurance. What is more, I only have to support myself. I am not rich down here, but I do have some disposable income. I can travel a little, and I eat out occasionally. The masons never eat out. We probably go out for a beer together once every couple of weeks. They count every quetzal and make sure their money goes as far as it can. These men have earned my respect. I am getting an invaluable education in principles and priorities down here.

Many of my Peace Corps days will be spent teaching and sharing my knowledge with others, but today is somehow different and more special. Today I give a few rudimentary math lessons at the Agua Para la Salud office. Five of the six guys I work with choose to attend. We work out various addition, subtraction, and multiplication problems. I showed the masons how to find the volume of a cylindrical tank, and I explain the difference between radius and circumference. We get a little sidetracked, so I also explain the difference between regular mail and electronic mail. If nothing else, the job of a PCV involves dealing with people. The masons I work with have received very little formal education. None of them can write well in Spanish. Yet they are so eager to learn. They thank me effusively at the end of the day; I leave the office without crying, but it is tough to hold those tears back. Yet again, I walk back to my house that afternoon deeply humbled.

Education is the key to individual empowerment. Nelson Mandela said, "Education is the most powerful weapon which you can use to change the world." I can do all the altruistic development work I want down here, and that still will be better than nothing. But the ultimate and lasting objective is to transfer knowledge and skills—to facilitate and preserve institutional knowledge. If I fail, I will not be alone, but I can't use that as an excuse. I am a coward if I do.

HALLOWEEN 2006: TODOS SANTOS

Today, I travel to Todos Santos, Huehuetenango. The journey from Nebaj should last about ten hours. A medley of *micros* (minivans) and camionetas will get me to my destination as unsafely as possible. I am going because today is October 31 and there is purportedly a solid Halloween Peace Corps party every year in Todos Santos. Besides, I don't have anything else going on. More importantly, on November 1 there will be drunken horse races to commemorate *el Día de los Muertos:* the Day of the Dead. Day of the Dead ceremonies in Mexico are far more famous, but this is still an important event in Guatemala, especially in small towns like Todos Santos. November 1 is meant to be a celebration of life, commemorating the deceased and the lives they lived. Many families will visit the local graveyard that morning, bringing flowers and candles. I have heard that local marimba bands meander through the graveyard and play songs upon request. Todos Santos is supposed to be a highly traditional place, like Nebaj. And November first is one of the most important days of the year. Me, on the other hand, I just want to see some drunken horse races and hang out with some of my Peace Corps buddies.

My weekend in Todos Santos is fun, but the actual horse races, the reason I went there, are underwhelming. All the indigenous men participating in those races are hammered. Most of them can barely walk, let alone ride a horse in what I mistakenly assumed was a competitive event. I am too worn-out from the Halloween party the night before to enjoy it anyway. I watch the spectacle from a nearby hill for about an hour and then walk back to the house we rented for the weekend. I need a nap. My head is throbbing. I hadn't expected it to be so hot; by the time I get back to my bed, my shirt is soaked through with sweat.

NOVEMBER 24, 2006: TURKEY DAY IN NAHUALÁ

It's Thanksgiving, and about fifteen people from my training group are in Nahualá to celebrate. The town is situated in the department of Sololá, just off the Inter-American Highway between Los Encuentros and Xela. I have a map in my bedroom that says Nahualá is the highest point on the Inter-American Highway.

Eric Schroeder and Carin Robinson, two of my good friends from training, both live here. Eric advises an Internet café on financial matters, and Carin works for the town's biggest radio station. They both seem to be enjoying themselves thus far.

Most of my colleagues bring prepared dishes to share. I have no culinary talent, so I just buy several boxes of Clos—Chilean boxed wine that cannot be purchased in town. I arrive at Carin's house at around two o'clock. Carin told me yesterday that we would eat at around three-thirty at Eric's. It looks like several people have already had quite a bit to drink. Carin and Eric are working the hardest. The party moves from Carin's to Eric's. We are all at Eric's house at four-fifteen to say the blessing. Carin shares a really cute limerick with the group. Then a few other people give mediocre speeches, and everyone starts to dig in. The food is excellent. Eric and Carin paid a Guatemalan in town to cook a huge turkey. The wine and beer are flowing. I am juggling three interesting conversations at once. Before I know it, Walker from Paris, Texas, is bringing out pumpkin pie. This is paradise.

We spend the rest of the day socializing, drinking, dancing, and just relaxing, enjoying each other's company. We have so much to be thankful for and, more importantly, we know it.

PART II

Six: Reconnect

"I don't know what your destiny will be, but one thing I know: the only ones among you who will be really happy are those who will have sought and found how to serve."

—*Dr. Albert Schweitzer*

November 27, 2006

Today my training group starts our three-day Peace Corps Reconnect at the training center. "Reconnect" is a time for a training group to get together again after having spent approximately three months in site. Peace Corps volunteers share their experiences with the members of their group, and people can express any concerns they might have about our remaining twenty-one months of service. As spokesman for our group, I also give a brief speech that the Peace Corps administration inaptly titles "Taylor Dibbert's Words of Wisdom." I speak self-deprecatingly about my first three months in site and include that fateful day when dozens of ants enjoyed my scrawny legs for breakfast. Additionally, I underscore the fact that we only have twenty months or six hundred days or 14,376 hours of service left after today. The first day goes relatively smoothly; I'm certainly happy to see some of my friends who now live on the other side of the country.

I'm staying with my former host family until Friday. After living at my site for three months, Santo Tomás looks like a swanky resort town. Everything seems so clean. The streets look neat and orderly. Can I really be thinking these thoughts? What is the Peace Corps doing to me?

DECEMBER 2, 2006

We celebrate our last day of Reconnect today. There's a keg at Jim's house in Santo Tomás. Jim is a middle-aged American living very close to the Peace Corps training center. He is a gregarious guy and loves to party. We roast a pig and Jim brings a couple of Gallo kegs. When the pig appears to be "done," everybody gets on their hands and knees and digs in. All of us are either half-drunk or completely wasted, and we're down on hands and knees, stuffing our faces with half-cooked pig. Guatemala has turned us all into animals. I feel like we're reenacting a chapter from *Lord of the Flies*.

DECEMBER 7, 2006: XELA

If you are a Peace Corps volunteer spending the night in Xela, then you are probably sleeping at Casa Argentina, one of the biggest and most popular hostels in town. The place is huge; there are probably forty-five rooms here, both private rooms and dorm rooms. Many of the rooms have television, and it's only 25Q for Peace Corps volunteers, which is excellent. There are three kitchens for people who want to do their own cooking, and there is a tap with filtered water. The hostel is run by a friendly Guatemalan family. Again, by American standards, the amenities are not impressive, but this is Guatemala. Casa Argentina is the ideal hostel for backpackers or anyone else who is traveling on a budget.

My meeting at COFA—the Catholic Family Retreat Center, a convent on the edge of the city—went well. The building was designed to hold spiritual retreats, but the Peace Corps frequently uses it for meetings. Basilio Estrada, my APCD (Associate Peace Corps Director—my boss) wants a few PCVs to help restructure the Appropriate Technology program, my program.

Evidently, an upper-level Peace Corps official working in the Dominican Republic wrote a lengthy and highly critical report about the Peace Corps Guatemala Appropriate Technology program. He thinks the program should focus more on health and hygiene education instead of infrastructure development.

Five PCVs and I dissected it today with Basilio. Additionally, Basilio told us today that Peace Corps Guatemala will be moving from a training-center based program to a community-based program. This is a big shake-up because it will dramatically alter the lives of incoming trainees. Basically, community-based training revolves around volunteers working and learning in their respective communities as much as possible, while avoiding the training center as much as possible. Conversely, our group spent seven to ten hours a day at the training center. We only returned home in the late afternoon. Ultimately it does not matter what I think, because this decision has been mandated by our new country director, Todd Sloan. Todd worked previously as a Peace Corps country director in Nicaragua and strongly feels that the community-based model is both more effective in terms of preparing trainees for their service and more efficient. It's hard for me to agree or disagree. I am only familiar with one of the two styles.

DECEMBER 8, 2006

Today I commemorate the twenty-fourth anniversary of my birth. Members of my immediate Guatemalan family (my friends in my training group) will come to Xela to help me celebrate accordingly. I am still full of the fervor of youth, or maybe it is just the fervor of life. I'm not sure. Regardless, I feel alive. Youth is enthusiasm. Youth is courage. Youth is deciding to actually take that road less traveled. Youth is that judicious angel guiding my every move.

Youth is freedom. Best of all, my seven months in the Peace Corps have taught me that I am not alone. There are more free spirits; I just have to keep searching in order to find them.

Our training group is trouble this weekend. I have come to realize that this is the norm and not an aberration. My good friend Eric Schroeder from Chicago definitely wins the contest for the most entertaining drunken miscue. That Friday night we spend several hours drinking at Tecun Uman, a very popular bar right in the heart of Xela, right off the Parque Centroamérica. Our boisterous group of twenty commandeers the entire bar upstairs. It is from that bar that PCV Eric Schroeder falls while trying to sing happy birthday to me for a second time. Eric makes a huge cracking sound when he hits the hardwood floor. His glasses even fly across the room. After that, the bartender refuses to dim the lights. Evidently, Eric damaged his glasses. Everyone breaks out laughing once they realize that he is okay. He got lucky, and so did the rest of us; he could have been badly injured. After seven hours of drinking, none of us is in good enough shape to handle the situation with equanimity.

DECEMBER 9, 2006: SATURDAY EVENING

Six of us are sitting at Casa Argentina drinking Clos boxed wine from Chile. We are trying to get rid of our hangovers from the night before. I don't think anyone is planning on going out.

As some like to say, "It's not great wine, but it's close." We have been playing cards and talking for several hours. Most of us have had quite a bit to drink. Somehow we started talking about lesbians.

"Have any of y'all ever made out with a girl before?"

"Why? Would that be weird to you?"

"Absolutely not."

"Yeah, that would just be awesome. Remember, we are guys. Lesbians are cool."

"I've never really thought about it. I'd do it for money."

"Seriously? How much money?"

"Are you paying?"

"Wait, ladies, I think we could raise a little money for this."

"Who would you make out with?"

"I don't know. Whoever."

"Okay, Carin should make out with Kara."

"I'll throw money down for that."

"Me too."

"Anybody else willing to put a few Q into the pot?"

Then the magic happens. Kara and Carin end up making out for what turns out to be sixty-nine quetzales, less than ten American dollars. Carin is more enthusiastic than Kara, and it shows once they start kissing. In my view, this is understandable, since Carin went to graduate school in the Netherlands. She is just more open-minded anyway. Man, I love the Peace Corps. And I love boxed wine.

DECEMBER 14, 2006

I am finishing the last days of 2006 in Nebaj without water and in complete solitude. For whatever reason, the pipes in my house burst this morning. I will be sans water until January, since Lynn has already left to see his family in the States. I guess I could always shower outside; the rain has not let up in the Ixil Triangle. Throughout most of Guatemala, the rainy season runs from May through August. Ixil country is different. Here it rains nearly year round. I have been told that there's little rain in February, March, and April. As of now, I don't know what to believe. I have already gone through two ponchos.

I have, in fact, become a master of solitude. This is not uncommon. In fact, what I am doing right now—staring at my ceiling—is so quintessentially Peace Corps that it's exhilarating. I have just finished a couple of peanut-butter sandwiches for lunch. Last week, I was pleasantly surprised to discover that wheat bread is sold in Nebaj. Most Ixils hate the stuff, but I can never get enough of it, especially since I am eating so many tortillas here. I need to make sure I eat enough fiber, otherwise I get constipated.

This had never been a problem before I came to Guatemala, but it's a concern now. With large quantities of rice, corn tortillas, and pasta, my diet revolves almost entirely around carbohydrates. Carbohydrates don't help me go to the bathroom. I've already had to take a laxative a few times. It's not a procedure I'm eager to repeat.

I have been learning about Paul Theroux's Peace Corps experience in his semiautobiographical work *My Secret History*. I absolutely cannot believe the guy had so much hassle-free sex in Central Africa. Theroux never even mentions sleeping with anyone but the locals. Conversely, I haven't slept with anyone for eight months now. In fact, I'll admit that I have not even been close to an "adult situation." I am pathetic. I am definitely better-looking than Theroux. What am I doing wrong?

I read some more of *My Secret History* and listen to the rain fall intermittently on my lamina porch. I burn incense like it will be my last day to do so. I am ready for my Christmas vacation in Nicaragua. I am ready to embrace the wisdom of uncertainty and the rhapsody of adventure. People, places, restaurants, culture, scenery—I will soak up the experience like a sponge. I will meticulously absorb all available knowledge. I won't sleep well tonight; I am too excited.

The following morning, I get to the Nebaj terminal early for a ride to Quiché. Bus terminals in Guatemala are a fascinating cultural experience. This is a place where I see a little bit of everything. Several comedores are nearby. Vendors are all over the place, selling all kinds of things. Right now I see people, mostly young boys, selling peanuts, newspapers, drinks, gum, candy, fruit, and ice cream. It's obvious that I'm a foreigner, so the five Guatemalans need to ask me where I'm going at least ten times. I tell them twenty times that I'm headed down to Quiché on my way to Guatemala City. They finally leave me alone. A few months later, people will start to recognize my face and leave me alone, realizing that I know what I'm doing.

When I get to Quiché, I quickly board another camioneta bound for "Guate." I will meet up with three other Peace Corps volunteers from my training group. We hope to grab a few hours of sleep in a seedy Zone 1 hotel tonight. Our bus leaves for Managua tomorrow morning at 5:00 a.m.

SEVEN: CHECK YOUR HEAD

JANUARY 8, 2007: BACK TO REALITY IN NEBAJ

I spent the past two weeks in Nicaragua with three friends from training: Carin, James, and Olivia. We went to the colonial town of Granada, the gorgeous island Ometepe, and the beach in San Juan del Sur. It was an amazing trip. Nicaragua is cheaper and poorer than Guatemala. The infrastructure there is even less developed than Guatemala's. On average, I thought the Nicaraguans were more attractive than the Guatemalans. And they were definitely taller. We refilled our water bottles in the sink all week. It's okay to drink the tap water in Nicaragua because of Lake Nicaragua, the enormous natural lake.

Before our vacation, I had made the mistake of conflating Nicaragua with my Peace Corps experience. My time in Nicaragua now feels quite different. Nicaragua was a separate entity. I live and work in Guatemala.

It feels weird and mildly depressing to be back in Nebaj. The stark reality has hit me: I live here. I live in a small indigenous village in a country that most of my compatriots would be hard-pressed to locate on a map. It's so cold and rainy in January, I may need some Xanax to get through this weather.

The rain has let up. I grab my trash can and carry it outside into the backyard. Then I grab a container of diesel and a pack of matches. I need to burn my trash. I should have done this before I left for Nicaragua, but it slipped my mind. Yes, I burn all my trash. I was concerned at first when Daniel told me that was what he did. But Lynn told me the same thing. At times, living in Guatemala is about choosing the best option among a variety of poor options. Many villagers dump their trash in lakes or rivers, which would be much worse. A little diesel makes this process go much more smoothly. As I listen to the intermittent crackling of the flames, I begin to daydream. My mind wanders aimlessly for the next fifteen minutes. Before I know it, I am staring at a pile of ashes. I grab a shovel and deposit the ashes in a pit a few yards away.

JANUARY 9, 2007

I'm eating a standard lunch at my house today: instant noodles with prepackaged tomato sauce and a banana for dessert. I read recently that Momofuku Ando, the creator of instant soup died. Born in Taiwan and raised in Japan, the man was trying to create a simple food that could be prepared easily. He was also hoping to feed a lot of people for very little money. PCVs around the world should mourn this guy's death. This man has wielded great influence over my daily life, first in college and now in the Peace Corps.

Like most of Latin America, Guatemala's history is rife with economic struggles and political turbulence and American interference. However, the country's most recent fiasco is different. I am not talking about exchange rates, unemployment statistics, or civil unrest. It's something much simpler this time. Those sagacious oracles running the Bank of Guatemala did not have the foresight to print enough money during the peak of the country's tourist season. There is no way to sugarcoat this; it should be viewed in the international press as an absolute embarrassment. If only Guatemala could *get* any attention from the international media. This impoverished place desperately needs revenue from tourism. Now I am forced to travel more than two hours to Quiché to get money. It's sort of funny, because the Peace Corps administration is so concerned with safety, and yet what could be more unsafe than not having any money?

I am reading *The Grapes of Wrath*, a terrific novel. Steinbeck talks about human-rights violations, forced migration, questionable labor practices, wage drops, abysmal working conditions, and more. Then it strikes me: this book could have hit the shelves yesterday, though the novel's setting would no longer be the United States. A country like Guatemala would be a more appropriate choice.

On my less productive days, I habitually indulge in idle daydreaming. My thoughts may even turn negative. I'll think about living in the middle of nowhere, reading a bunch of stories, eating copious amounts of bananas, and drinking plastic bags full of water. I think about how I'm twenty-four, but living in Guatemala makes me feel like a withered old man. I'm not alone. I'm lonely. Most days I turn to my journal to vent. I have even written my first article for the Peace Corps Guatemala newsletter, the *Id*.

JANUARY 12, 2007

I have meetings scheduled all morning starting at 8:00 a.m. to discuss future water projects. By 8:30 a.m., they have all been cancelled. I decide to remain at the office and read another Peace Corps-issued copy of *Newsweek*, a publication that has disappointed me so far. Why couldn't they have given us a subscription to the *Economist?* So what if it's British? I go back to my house and watch a little CNN *en español*. I have a crush on one of their lead anchors, Colombian heartthrob Claudia Palacios.

CNN is the only decent channel out of the six we get. Though I've never been a big television fan, I was pleasantly surprised to discover that I had access to a small one. I will have loads of free time, and it could be good for my Spanish. I can already tell that I'm going to have a difficult time improving in that area while in

Nebaj. To be fair, the Ixils speak Spanish as a second language also. In Nebaj, many of the men speak well, but the majority of women do not. There is a noticeable difference among the younger people. Almost all of them, including girls, speak Spanish well. It's different in the villages outside Nebaj. The women usually can only speak a few words of Spanish. While most of the men in the most rural areas can speak it, it's usually quite rudimentary and oftentimes grammatically incorrect.

JANUARY 23, 2007

Today I am in San Antonio Ilotenango (southern Quiché) for a medical mission with Compañeros en Salud. A guy named David Laserwitz runs their program now; he called me a couple weeks ago. David finished his service as a Peace Corps volunteer in Guatemala and then started working for this group. He was wondering if I was available as a translator. I told him I was, and that I looked forward to meeting him.

I have never done this type of work before. It is an eye-opener. Hundreds of villagers come from all over southern Quiché. Most of the people hear about this sort of thing on the radio. Upon arrival, they each take a number and wait patiently in line. Compañeros en Salud works with doctors in the United States and Canada. These medical missions are preliminary screenings. If possible, certain people will be scheduled for low-risk surgeries within a year, with cleft palates and hernias being the most common problems.

I see a hernia the size of a grapefruit. How long had this guy had the thing? About a year, he tells me. Wow. I could never be that tough; I probably would have jumped off a bridge by then. I have only been down here about six months, but my own health issues now seem so minor. How can I complain about a receding hairline or acid reflux? Those are such trivial issues.

JANUARY 25, 2007

This morning, Diego and I are confronted by Agua Para el Pueblo and its corrupt practices for the first time. Before today, I had heard of them, but I didn't know much about them. They are a Guatemalan NGO collaborating with the United Nations and other international donors. They charge about $100,000 for a water system that should only cost $20,000. Diego and I visit several villages that morning. We are trying to ascertain whether they are still interested in building a water system in their town. That's when a community leader in one of the villages, Tujulom Grande, shows us an Agua Para el Pueblo budget. I can't believe my eyes. All of their material costs are grossly inflated. On the sheet for administrative costs, they are going to charge the community 100,000 quetzales just for organizing meetings. I would hope an organization like the UN would never knowingly go along with this corruption, but they don't always do their homework. Or maybe most of the upper-level bureaucrats are corrupt. Clearly they don't always check to make sure that their money is being spent properly. Sadly, there is a lot of money in poverty.

FEBRUARY 6, 2007

The ATMs in Nebaj are out of money again! This is unbelievable. I'll probably have to ride down to Quiché next week to get money. That's a waste of an entire afternoon, because it takes me two hours to get there. I'm sure Lynn would let me borrow some money, but I don't know how much cash he has. (A note: Quiché is the name of a department in Guatemala, but in this context, and many others, I am referring to Santa Cruz del Quiché—the capital city of the department, which people refer to merely as Quiché.)

FEBRUARY 12, 2007

I drive up to El Mirador with Diego to explain my SPA (Small Project Assistance) proposal. We have perfect weather; I can see for miles through my passenger-side window. I love riding in our "company car," a light green 1961 Toyota Land Cruiser. The vehicle belongs in an automotive history museum.

SPA projects are approved on a case-by-case basis; these projects are funded through the US Agency for International Development. SPA projects are only approved after a PCV swims across an ocean of red tape. Frankly, the process seems so convoluted that I would be surprised if I ever successfully complete one. Nevertheless, I can at least plan a project to be completed in El Mirador. And if the SPA committee doesn't come through for me, at least I will have a complete project proposal to show some groups or individuals who have helped me fund other projects.

Like a lot of indigenous villages in the western highlands, the history of El Mirador is a disheartening one. At the peak of Guatemala's civil war in the early 1980s, the violence in the Ixil Triangle was widespread. Many villagers fled across the border to Mexico. Only after the peace accords were signed in 1996 did villagers slowly start to return. El Mirador is a community of former refugees. This morning, it took Diego and me two hours to drive out there. Diego and I are becoming close friends, so I never mind a long car ride with him. We never talk about anything in particular. He might tell me about his amigos or relatives living in the United States. I might tell him what I did last weekend. He might have a cultural question or two about Texas. I might ask him about Ixil women. He might wonder if I am homesick yet. I might ask him about politics in Nebaj. The possibilities are not endless, but we have plenty to talk about.

FEBRUARY 13, 2007: BATZAJA

I spend the entire day with Diego in Batzaja. We are correcting a water survey completed by a Frenchman named Gildas who worked with Agua Para la Salud over a year ago. One of the most negative aspects of working at Agua Para la Salud is that many times, volunteers or development workers will leave before one of their projects has been completed—meaning that others are left to interpret their work for the masons and community members.

If they have made no mistakes, then there is no problem. But if there are any errors, a project becomes exponentially more complicated.

Thank God I am able to remember enough of Neruda's poetry, especially his *Veinte Poemas de Amor y una Canción Desesperada*, to get me through the day. Walt Whitman is also with me. I like *Leaves of Grass*. Occasionally a water survey can get boring after several hours. As Diego and I walk back to the car, I feel my cheeks burning. I must have gotten quite a bit of sun today.

FEBRUARY 14, 2007

February, March, and April are the driest months of the year in Nebaj. This coincides with the driest part, the undisputed nadir, of my already disappointing romantic career. I am celebrating another loveless Valentine's Day. What is worse, I've never even been close to being in love. Love eludes me at every turn. Love laughs in my face. Love is a mystery to me. I'm starting to think the same thing about sex. I am an island. As a Peace Corps volunteer, I am making a few sacrifices.

Today, Diego and I conduct some health surveys in Batzaja. By that, I mean that Diego conducts the surveys in Ixil, and I tag along and work as a scribe. On the way back to the car, we spot some gorgeous avocado trees. Manuel, the community president, is walking with us and suggests we go grab a few avocadoes to complement our evening meal. Once we get close, I assume we are wasting our time; the avocadoes are too high up. How are we going to reach them? Simple answer: machetes. Before long, Diego, Manuel, and I are launching our machetes into the air. Of course, Diego and Manuel toss those blades with more dexterity than me, but I hold my own. Twenty minutes later, Diego and I drive off with two backpacks full of avocadoes—exhausted, sunburned, and poised for whatever challenges tomorrow will bring.

I'm reading Kafka's *Amerika*, and I am suddenly hit with a paroxysm of introspection. I realize that I have lived in Guatemala for nearly ten months. I've met some incredible people and almost frozen to death in the mountains. I've learned how to work with cement. I have become a bona fide development worker. I've read over eighty books, spoken in front of a large group at the US ambassador's house, picked up some cool nicknames, and spent Christmas in Nicaragua. I've been mauled by fire ants and gotten a root canal. It's been an incredible journey, and I've still got a year and a half left.

FEBRUARY 17, 2007

Today I reflect upon the work of a few literary masters. The myriad sacrifices that writers have made while honing their craft invigorates me. Kafka worked in a government insurance office for many years and wrote at the same time. All of his major works were published posthumously. J. M. Coetzee worked as a computer programmer and a linguist. He also did some aimless wandering through the streets of London in his early twenties. T. S. Eliot worked at Lloyd's bank. And Conrad didn't attempt to write until he had traveled the world. I could go on, but I won't. Privations must be accepted for greatness to materialize. Am I one of the chosen? I realize that the odds are against me. I am not special. I am not bound for literary greatness, yet I cling to a tiny thread of hope. Unconvinced that anyone will ever read a word of it, I press on and continue to write.

MARCH 4, 2007

This morning I read *The World Is Flat*. After doing so, I want to rush over to the nearest Internet café and download business-school applications. Instead, I head to the Nebaj market. Unfortunately, it's raining—which means that the market is even more disgusting than usual. I have lived in town long enough that most vendors know not to lie to me about prices. This gringo knows his prices. When I travel, I still get lied to about the cost of transportation, but as soon as I tell the *ayudante*, the person who collects the fares, that I live in Guatemala, he normally backs down. Guatemalans, especially indigenous Guatemalans, do not like confrontation.

After all this, I feel nothing except acute loneliness. That's when I break out the phone list and call several friends back home. And lastly, I call my parents. Ninety-nine percent of Peace Corps volunteers have cell phones. I have yet to meet a PCV who doesn't have one. Placing calls to landlines in the United States is not that expensive; it costs about a quetzal per minute, less than ten cents. But it's significantly more costly if I call a cell phone back home. Sundays in Nebaj are the most languid, utterly listless days in the Western Hemisphere.

MARCH 12, 2007

I have been working with and also training my colleague, Diego Ramírez, since I arrived in Nebaj. This has been my only experience with adult education in the Third World. Diego is a highly skilled mason, great public speaker, and outstanding leader at Agua Par la Salud. He never received much in the way of formal education, but he even speaks some English. The guy is the smartest person I have met in Nebaj by far, although Diego sometimes disappoints me. Today he admits that he doesn't know the Spanish alphabet or understand the purpose of a dictionary. This is followed by his nonchalantly declaring that the English alphabet is the same as the Spanish one. I let him down gently.

"Pues Taylor, confío en ti. Si me dices que no es verdad. Entonces estoy de acuerdo."

"Vaya, amigo."

"Es que. A veces, uno se confunde."

"Claro, podría pasarle a cualquier persona."

"Y Taylor, yo sé algo de los Estados. Aunque nunca he estado allí."

"¿Y qué es lo que sabes?"

"Que allí Ustedes hacen bien el estudio."

"Le digo que tiene razón."

"Taylor, I trust you. If you tell me that's not true, I will believe you."

"Okay, buddy."

"It's just that, sometimes, one gets confused."

"Sure, it could happen to anybody."

"And Taylor, I know something about the States. Although I've never been there."

"And what is it that you know?"

"You all have a really good educational system."

"You are right about that."

APRIL 13, 2007

Slow Man by Coetzee forces me to focus on the issues of true importance in life—namely the notion that disability, even in its most mild state, sucks. I cannot imagine what it would be like to sleep with a blind woman I've never met. I cannot imagine ever having sex blindfolded like Coetzee's flawed protagonist Paul Rayment. In fact, right now I can't imagine myself ever having sex again under any circumstances. Occasionally, I see a cute tourist wandering around town, but she's usually traveling with a male companion. It doesn't really matter, because I'm not sure that I would have the courage to hit on someone under those circumstances anyway. I just hope I am able to last the full twenty-seven months.

EIGHT: THE ROAD TO NOWHERE

"If you are going through hell, keep going."
—*Winston Churchill*

APRIL 23, 2007

I feel bored and frustrated with Guatemala. I don't want to eat any more tortillas. I'm sick of all the noise. I don't understand why people listen to their music with the volume cranked all the way up. I'm sick of waking up to firecrackers outside my house in Nebaj. That happens at least once a week. I'm sick of using hand sanitizer eight times a day. I'm sick of getting sick. I already feel like my time in this country has taken ten years off my life. My work at Agua Para la Salud has become monotonous; the job has lost its luster. My once limitless curiosity has waned. I am nowhere near the end or the beginning of my service—just hanging tough in the Third World. I am still waiting for that indescribable epiphany, the moment after which I can state with absolute certainty the following words: *Yes, I did the Peace Corps, and it was worth it.*

This afternoon at an Internet café, I read an odd BBC news article. Apparently, the lovely Sheryl Crow is recommending that people use only one square of toilet paper per bathroom visit or maybe two because that is the correct, environmentally conscious decision. She also proposes that people wear a "removable napkin sleeve" instead of using real napkins. Obviously, the lovely Miss Crow has never been to Guatemala. If she had visited this country, she would know that her seemingly helpful suggestions are utterly impractical. Diarrhea is an integral part of daily life here. In spite of Miss Crow's naive suggestions, I still have a huge crush on her and love her music.

MAY 8, 2007

This afternoon, Agua Para la Salud employees Diego Ramírez and Dionysio Gaspar got robbed outside of Acul, a quaint village a few miles west of Nebaj. They told me there were five *ladrones* (thieves). Later, Diego said that one of the other men who got robbed was crying and then wet his pants and then passed out, Bible in hand. Diego then strapped the guy to the back of a motorcycle and rode to the local hospital to get him checked out. Diego also told me that the ladrones all had M-16 assault rifles, which I believe were gifts of the Reagan administration.

Today, Ronald Reagan is venerated for winning the Cold War. Many conservatives will wrongly claim that Reagan was a champion of human rights. This claim is misleading at best. Yes, Ronald Reagan did some good things during his presidency. But his errors in Latin America and, more specifically, Central America are rarely acknowledged. In fact, Reagan was a stalwart defender of military regimes. He consistently overlooked the egregious human-rights violations that those regimes committed. I am not talking about segregated buses or bathrooms, but the rape, murder, and torture of mostly indigenous peasants on a massive scale. Without question, what happened in Guatemala was genocide.

Efraín Ríos Montt led a "scorched-earth" campaign in the early 1980s. His seventeen months in power are widely regarded as the darkest days of Guatemala's civil war. But not for Ronald

Reagan, who said that Ríos Montt was "a man of great personal integrity." Ríos Montt is a monster. Period. The man has a heart of stone. And he should be tried for war crimes.

In 1999, a United Nations-sponsored truth commission determined that the military was responsible for 93 percent of the human-rights violations, while the guerrillas were responsible for only 3 percent of the atrocities. Furthermore, this Historical Clarification Commission said that the military had committed hundreds of massacres, 626 to be exact, of indigenous villages in the 1980s. Two hundred thousand people died in Guatemala's thirty-six-year civil conflict. Estimates say that over a million people were displaced. In the country's western highlands, many villages still have not recovered.

Unfortunately, Guatemala was not the only country in Central America where Reagan backed a ruthless, unjust counterinsurgency. Reagan was capable of anything in the name of fighting communism. The US government also dumped hundreds of millions of dollars into both Nicaragua and El Salvador. I will not elaborate upon US intervention in these countries. As an American, suffice it to say that our extensive involvement brings me great shame and disappointment.

MAY 9, 2007

I am enjoying a weekend in Monterrico. My training group decided to commemorate our one-year anniversary in country with a trip to the preeminent beach spot on Guatemala's sweltering Pacific coast. That's not saying much. We take a camioneta south to a place called La Avellana. From La Avellana, we take a small *lancha* over to Monterrico. When we arrive at Monterrico, I am sure we are in the wrong place. There isn't anything to see. There are a few old houses next to the dock and a bunch of men hollering at us, telling us they will take the *americanos* to the best hotel in town. I quickly ask a local where the hotel Johnny's is. We spend the next ten minutes wandering around and eventually find it.

I have never been to a beach with black sand. It's so hot here that I have to run every time I want to enter the water in order to avoid burning my feet. And I am perspiring like crazy. I've got to be more careful when I wipe the sweat from my face; I got sunscreen in my left eye last time. I think those are the angriest waves I have ever seen. I don't even swim out very far because I am afraid that the water will snap my neck in two. That night, my friend James Schintz and I meet a couple of "dancers" at a shady hotel bar on the water. These "dancers" say they will give us whatever we want. It is at this point that I notice the huge sack of weed on the table next to ours. One of the women tells me that I am very handsome, and that she will give me some "dancing lessons" in private if I am really interested. I impatiently tell her that I don't dance. James and I buy a couple beers for the road and get out of there. On the way back, we discuss drug use and how prevalent it is among Peace Corps volunteers.

If the Peace Corps actually cared about enforcing its antidrug policy, then the Peace Corps administration would test PCVs occasionally, though it doesn't do this. If there were drug testing for PCVs, Peace Corps Guatemala would easily lose around 80 percent of its volunteers. During my time as a PCV, I would learn that half of all volunteers smoke weed on a regular basis, and well over three-quarters of all volunteers smoke occasionally. There is also a little cocaine use, but it's more sporadic. All this is even more understandable given that high-quality drugs are relatively cheap in this country. A gram of cocaine would cost around a hundred quetzales, less than fifteen American dollars. A gram of decent coke in the United States would cost at least fifty bucks and sometimes much more. Weed is also vastly cheaper in Guatemala compared to the United States.

Drugs are most easily bought in Antigua and around Lake Atitlán, Sololá. (I assume there are plenty of drugs in the capital, but I haven't personally heard anything about Peace Corps volunteers buying any there.)

The best spot to buy drugs is San Pedro la Laguna. San Pedro is right on the water, so the view of the volcanoes surrounding the lake is gorgeous. Food and drinks are not as expensive as they are in Antigua. The nightlife is interesting but can get sketchy at times. San Pedro has a much more bohemian feel than Antigua. If you are a Westerner taking the *lancha* from the Panajachel dock, there is a 95 percent chance that people will offer you drugs before you've even gotten off the dock. San Pedro has been declared a restricted site by the Peace Corp administration, meaning that PCVs are not allowed to go there. Peace Corps administrators officially claim that this is because the area is not safe. Nothing could be further from the truth. They don't want volunteers to go to San Pedro because it's so easy to get cheap, high-quality drugs there. Furthermore, San Pedro is like Barcelona—it turns into a different place at night, where things can get funky in a hurry. Before you know it, you might be sharing a dorm room with some creepy people strung out on acid or heroin.

MAY 18, 2007

Diego and I drive up to speak with a few community leaders in several villages today. I am still annoyed with myself about forgetting my poncho, a rookie mistake. I will probably be soaked by the time we drive back to Nebaj. He soberly tells me that the ladrones hit again yesterday; this time, they robbed a camioneta near Xepiun. The police are never going to catch these guys.

This afternoon, Diego and I see some extraordinarily dishonest budgets in Tujolom Grande, yet another benighted village outside of Nebaj. Building a gravity-flow water system can be a long and arduous process, but again, there are parameters with regard to costs. Apparently, the corrupt mayor of Nebaj, Pap Xel, has been working with INFOM, a Guatemalan NGO. It's sad and terribly disappointing that in an area so rife with poverty, some educated Guatemalans don't hesitate to take advantage of the least fortunate. As previously stated, I have seen a similar budget done by Agua Para el Pueblo, another Guatemalan NGO. A gravity-flow water system does not cost 1.3 million quetzales. Even an expensive one should cost no more than 250,000Q, or $20,000.

May 20, 2007

This weekend, several State Department bureaucrats are visiting the Ixil Triangle. They will be sleeping in Nebaj for two nights. One of the Peace Corps administrative assistants called me earlier in the week to explain the situation.

"Hey Taylor, it's Lydia, how is everything in Nebaj?"

"Fine, Lydia, how are you doing?"

"Muy bien, gracias. Oye Taylor, necesito decirte algo."

"Okay, Lydia, what's up?"

"Listen, Taylor, next week, there will be four people from the US State Department visiting Nebaj. They will be in town for two nights, and they want to have dinner with a few Peace Corps volunteers. They said that they have chosen to visit Nebaj because it was such an important place during the civil war."

"Okay Lydia, so what do I need to do?"

"Nothing really, we would just like for you and the other three Peace Corps volunteers living in the area to have dinner with them, preferably on Friday night. Does that sound okay? Of course, this is optional. They'd like for you all to pick the restaurant."

"Okay, Lydia. That sounds good. I'll let Chris, Jeff, and Gloria know."

"Thanks so much, Taylor. Que tengas buen día."

"Vaya Lydia, está bien."

That afternoon, I call David Lindwell, the number-two man at the US embassy in Guatemala, and arrange for us to meet up that Friday at 7:00 p.m. Mr. Lindwell sounds like a genuinely nice man; I am looking forward to meeting him. They are staying at the Villa Nebaj, the fancy hotel in town. Fancy in Nebaj is not the same as fancy in the United States. The rooms at the Villa Nebaj are small. The beds are uncomfortable. The showers are decent as long as they aren't broken. The Villa Nebaj looks similar to a

Motel 6 in the United States. Anyway, I told Mr. Lindwell that we would meet his group in the lobby and then go to dinner.

All but one of them currently work at the US embassy in Guatemala City. The other man, Bill, a key player on the State Department's Policy Planning Staff, flew in from DC for the weekend.

Diplomatic dining in Nebaj feels more like a Foreign Service oral exam. It is clear that Bill is the key guy; he works on the same floor as Condi Rice. He just arrived in country today and boy, is he socially awkward—though he had lived in Lisbon, Paris, and Florence as a diplomat. It felt like the man came prepared with a list of specific questions. Big Bill is sitting to my right. In front of me is Mordica Simpson, young and quite attractive. She is a graduate of Yale and Johns Hopkins. This is only her second two-year tour in the Foreign Service. Sadly, she has just told me that she spends all her time processing visa applications. That's too depressing for me to comment on. I knew it was going to be a long night when nobody ordered booze out of the gate. I blame this entirely on my good friend Chris, since David Lindwell looked right at him when he asked what everyone would like to drink. Chris said *agua pura*, and the rest of our table followed suit.

After fending off Bill's questions for what seems like an eternity, I cautiously draw the conclusion that he is a Democrat. Now I am even more confused, since he is a senior-level guy at the State Department's Policy Planning Staff. I think that used to be Paul Wolfowitz's operation. I expected Bill to be a bit more hawkish. I'm surprised Bill hasn't been thrown out of an office window by now. I don't question the man's intelligence. I simply cannot imagine working with the guy.

Bill confirms my suspicions by abandoning his previous diatribe about fermenting homemade wine to segue into a conversation he had with Teresa Heinz Kerry. Bill got so excited when he mentioned her name, I thought he was going to say that he railed lines of coke with her at a Duran Duran concert in the late 1980s. Or that he made out with her at a United Nations fundraiser in

New York City. Maybe they were lovers. How could I have been so optimistic? Yet again, Bill is a huge disappointment.

"And so I introduced myself. And we were speaking to each other ... and we were switching back and forth between Brazilian and European Portuguese ... because I used to live in Lisbon ... so I know Portuguese. It really was crazy."

Sure Bill, you're a star. Chris, Gloria, Jeff, and I walk them back to the Villa Nebaj, say our good-byes, and go back to my house. After all, we have just endured a pretty tedious dinner. The alcohol-free aspect only added to the tedium. Equally disappointing was the fact that those Foreign Service people have absolutely no idea what Peace Corps volunteers do, not even a clue. I spent most of my time at dinner answering the most rudimentary questions. No, I have not seriously considered a career in the Foreign Service. No, I did not pick Guatemala for my Peace Corps service. That's not possible; prospective Peace Corps applicants can only denote a preference for a specific region. No, the Guatemalans I work with do not want to discuss American foreign policy. Most of the people I work with don't know what the words "foreign policy" mean.

Yes, I read a lot of books. Yes, now is a pretty introspective time for me. Yes, I have other friends who are also Peace Corps volunteers. Yes, I work in sites more isolated than Nebaj; that's where the neediest people are. Yes, everyone in Nebaj has water. Yes, Nebaj is a small town, about fifteen thousand people live here. Yes, the villages are much, much smaller. Yes, I work with a local NGO. And yes, I eat the local food. Otherwise I would be starving.

Nine: Visiban, Salquil, Quiché, and Quejchip

May 25, 2007: Visiban

Four of the masons and I will sleep in Visiban this week. Visiban is a village about two hours north of Nebaj. A few hundred people currently live there. It's right next to another village, El Mirador. Agua Para la Salud will build about three dozen 2,000-liter ferro-cement tanks over the next few months. I'll be helping the masons out this week, but they don't need me. Most of my time will be spent mixing cement and refilling their buckets with cement whenever necessary.

As always, we have hired a cook to prepare our meals. The cook is usually responsible for making breakfast, lunch, and dinner. This time, our cook Ana is quite young—either twelve or thirteen. She isn't sure which. She earns 70Q a week for doing this, which is a fair price out here. She is shy, and understandably so. Most of the women in her position would be timid anyway, but she is a child. She's not even sixteen, and already she's probably worked harder than I ever will. I have yet to see her wear shoes. She says it takes her twenty minutes to walk here from her parents' house. That can't be easy. After dinner every night, she meticulously cleans the dishes. She wishes us goodnight. Tonight is no different.

"Buenas noches, hasta mañana."

"Vaya, gracias por la cena. Estuvo bien."

Then she slips out of the room, tiny candle in hand. She is just a kid. She has her whole life ahead of her. Sadly, there are limitations. Ana is illiterate. She doesn't even speak much Spanish. She and her family are mired in poverty. This is the only life she'll ever know. I finish my tea and search for my toothbrush. Sleep would not come easy tonight.

MAY 26, 2007

My site mate, Chris, and I got drunk at Nebaj's only pool hall last night. After 10:00 p.m., and especially on the weekends, the place looks like a circus; half the men in there can't formulate coherent sentences. Some of the locals had already passed out in chairs by the time we arrived, while others were playing cards and smoking cigarettes. Of course there are no women anywhere near the place. An indigenous girl would do irreparable damage to her reputation if she were found in this pool hall, or any other bar for that matter. Strangely, the guys from Nebaj prefer to wear a pair of mittens while they are shooting pool. This is customary among Guatemalan pool players, but I had never seen it before. It seems childish.

Chris and I leave a little after midnight. On our way back, we see different couples making out in the street, taking advantage of the shadows. This is typical. Again, privacy is hard to come by in most of Guatemala. At home, these young people have very little of it. Enjoying an intimate moment in the street is sometimes easier than doing that at home. Interestingly, I witnessed the same behavior in Spain when I lived there.

JUNE 5, 2007

I spent the weekend in Antigua with friends. There was no special occasion; we were just meeting up to escape the reality of our respective sites. Antigua is overflowing with tourists in the summer. Last night I went to La Bodegona, a nice grocery store near the bus terminal, to pick up a few cans of Heineken and a gallon of water. As I was waiting in line I heard German, French, Italian, and an unidentifiable Asian language being spoken. This was all in a span of four or five minutes.

I'm now riding up to Nebaj with Lynn; two Peace Corps Spanish teachers; the Appropriate Technology trainer, David Castillo; and the fifteen new Appropriate Technology trainees. They have been in country for about a month.

Their field-based training will be held in Salquil Grande and Nebaj. This is primarily because Lynn has coordinated everything. Lynn has asked me to help out with the training. I will be leading a water survey near Salquil Grande and helping out in any way I can aside from that.

The training schedule that Lynn has planned is far more organized than my normal life in Nebaj. I had forgotten how structured and tedious Peace Corps training is. Aside from that, I am excited about meeting new and interesting people. It is usually entertaining to spend time with a group of overzealous Peace Corps trainees. I was in the same precarious position exactly one year ago. I had the same doubts, fears, and anxieties. Nothing makes me feel more like a seasoned veteran than speaking with newcomers.

JUNE 10, 2007

We have come back to Nebaj for one night to break up the work schedule, and all of us need a shower. The trainees will be sleeping at Don's, but Lynn has invited everyone over to his house for dinner that evening. No one can believe that I rent a room there for a paltry 300Q a month. I should be paying twice that amount. Lynn lives upstairs and uses a separate entrance. It's a perfect arrangement. I'll probably stay here until I finish my service.

Over the years, Lynn has befriended David Stoll, an American anthropologist who has done extensive research in Guatemala. His book *Between Two Armies* recounts and analyzes the history of Guatemala's civil war in the Ixil Triangle. In my opinion, it's the most important historical book that any American has ever written on the subject. In spite of its proximity to the United States, Guatemala gets little attention in the international media. News from indigenous villages in Guatemala is rarely mentioned in any widely read newspaper or magazine. People prefer to ignore the plight of the indigenous. Sometimes, ignoring reality is easier than facing the facts.

I am eating at a table with Dr. Stoll and PCV site mate Chris Mullen. Dr. Stoll is a very approachable man. At times he seems disoriented; I think that is only because he always has so much on his mind. I take this opportunity to ask him a few questions. I sorely miss the intellectual vibe of academia. There's a lot of intelligent conversation among PCVs, but none of us are professors or purported experts.

"So, Dr. Stoll …"

"You guys, please call me David."

"Okay, so David, are you working on anything right now? What brings you back to Nebaj?"

"Well, it's such an interesting place. I like to come back every now and then. My new thing is migration."

"Migration?"

"Yeah, I am researching migration, Guatemalans going to the US. I don't know if it will eventually become a book or not."

"Interesting. Do you mind if I ask you a couple other questions?"

"Not at all. I would be happy to answer them."

"Okay. So, obviously you have researched this area extensively. And there were egregious human-rights violations up here, some of the worst during the civil war. But how does that compare elsewhere? Do you think the Ixils were hit the hardest? Or were there other places where the indigenous people fared even worse? What town was hit the hardest in you opinion?"

"Yeah, people around here got it pretty bad. If I had to pick one place, I would say Panzos in Baja Verapaz."

"The location of the famous massacre in 1978?"

"That's right."

"Was anyone ever held legally responsible for that?"

"No."

"That sounds about right for this country."

Dr. Stoll has been teaching at Middlebury College in Vermont since 1997. He tells us that he will be on sabbatical next year. Hopefully this isn't my last conversation with this affable and engaging man.

JUNE 16, 2007

Toward the end of the field-based training, my APCD, Basilio Estrada, asks if I have considered extending my service for an additional year to be a Peace Corps volunteer leader. A PCV leader is a third-year volunteer. PCV leaders have more responsibility than regular PCVs. It's an honor to be invited, since he only extends one or two invitations per year. Basically, he wants me to be his personal assistant. I just don't know if I'm interested. Twenty-seven months may be enough for me. I thank him for his offer and tell him that I will consider it. Do I want to stay here for another year?

JUNE 18, 2007

Today I was going to finalize some budgets for upcoming projects at the office. Unfortunately, the power has been out since 6:30 a.m. The power frequently goes out when it rains, but we have had clear skies in Nebaj all day. It will probably come back on after 5:00 p.m. like it usually does. This happens a lot in Guatemala. When there is a shortage of electricity, the Spanish power company Unión Fenosa will cut the power in the less affluent parts of the country, where people use less power anyway. In Nebaj, many times the power will come back on between 5:00 p.m. and 7:00 p.m., since people in Guatemala City or Xela have finished working for the day. In the eyes of electricity giant Unión Fenosa, the people in the Ixil Triangle don't matter.

JUNE 22, 2007

I am in Quiché today to give a presentation. My meeting doesn't start until ten o'clock, so I have time to continue reading *Watt* in my seedy hotel. I read a few of Samuel Beckett's plays in high school, but this is my first experience with one of his novels. I have heard that *Watt* is one of his most accessible works. Many times Beckett makes me laugh. He's such a clever writer. Other times, I feel like I'm lost in a sarcastic labyrinth, hopping around on one foot while blindfolded, trying to grasp the Irishman's most abstruse assertions.

Later that morning, I speak to approximately fifty Guatemalan health promoters. I explain some of my responsibilities as a Peace Corps volunteer working with Agua Para la Salud. Monica, a fellow Appropriate Technology volunteer based in Huehuetenango, also gives a speech. All the health promoters present are thinking about petitioning for a PCV in their respective towns next year. Associate Peace Corps Director Basilio Estrada speaks briefly before Monica and me. The day is deemed a success, and Basilio thanks me and Monica for coming. I've never thought of myself as a strong public speaker, but that is beginning to change. I've had to speak in public on numerous occasions since I arrived in Guatemala a little more than a year ago. With each additional speech, I feel more and more comfortable. The Peace Corps is forcing me to improve. This is a useful skill that I will have for the rest of my life.

JUNE 25, 2007: QUEJCHIP

Diego and I are conducting a water survey in Quejchip, two hours away from Nebaj by car. Once again, I spent most of last night on the toilet, but we had planned this water survey weeks ago. I had to be there. I thought I had gotten it all out of my system; I was wrong.

"Diego, ¿puede escribir Usted por un ratito?"

"Si, claro. ¿Adónde vas tú?"

"Estoy malo. Voy al baño. Regreso enseguida."

"Vaya."

"Diego, could you write for a few minutes?"

"Yeah, sure. Where are you going?"

"I'm not feeling well. I'm going to the bathroom. I'll be right back."

"Okay."

We are right in the middle of an open field, so I take off jogging. Within minutes, I locate a more remote area on a hillside and, hugging a tree for balance, I find some much-needed relief. Luckily, I remembered to bring a roll of toilet paper that morning.

As I am cleaning myself up, I begin to suspect that the spot I chose was not remote enough. I think I hear someone laughing from afar. I pull up my pants and slowly turn around. Four kids had been hiding behind a pair of cows. They had seen everything.

"¿Todo bien gringo? ¿Estás malo del estómago o qué?"

"Sí, claro que sí pero gracias por preguntar."

"¿Te vas?"

"Sí, hay que trabajar. No hemos terminado todavía."

"Vaya pues, adiós."

"Is everything alright gringo? Do you have an upset stomach or what?"

"Yeah. I'm fine, but thanks for asking."

"You are going?"

"Yes, I have to work. We haven't finished yet."

"Okay then, bye."

I still hear laughter as I walk off. I don't feel too embarrassed; at least I didn't go in my pants. Besides, finding relief in the mountains is a memorable experience.

Ten: Unconquered

"I am the master of my fate: I am the captain of my soul."

—*William Ernest Henley*

Adoption

Since I came to Guatemala, my views on two subjects have changed dramatically: adoption and immigration. I will touch on immigration later. As for adoption, theoretically it is mostly a good thing. But that's not what I'm thinking today.

I am grabbing a bite to eat at the Rainbow Café in Antigua. I only want to devour my chicken quesadilla and hit the road. After eating, I must ride a chicken bus for seven hours back to Nebaj, so I try to enjoy my last relaxing moments of the day, to no avail. Three women with two massive strollers seat themselves at the table adjacent to mine. I brace myself for the worst. Out of nowhere, another potential mom approaches. This one arrives sans massive stroller. And so it begins.

"Oh hey, how are you?"

"Hey you, top of the morning! I'm just fantastic, thanks. How are you doing?"

One of the stroller ladies is screaming, which is so unnecessary. Generally, exaggerated voice inflections are unnecessary too.

"Is this your friend?"

"Sure is, in fact, well, get ready, we're both adopting!"

New mom number two screams now. These women sound like children.

"This is just *so* much fun!"

"*So* fun! I'm *so* happy for you two. They are such cute babies. I mean good for you guys, you know, not everyone can you know, like, adopt. And look, they're such cute little babies!"

I don't even finish my food. I throw some money on the table and head for the bus terminal.

Why did I choose Rainbow? I love the food, but it's usually crowded on Sundays. Should I have known better? It's hard to believe, but Guatemala currently ranks number one in total adoptions to the United States annually. China and then Russia follow behind this Central American country. Attention: these statistics are not based on per capita terms, but the total number of adoptions per country. This is scary stuff.

In fact, there was recently a big scandal at a house in Antigua. Apparently, Guatemalans had been stealing babies from indigenous villages with impunity and then selling them to desperate North American families. It's a sad story. Next week, the US government will put an indefinite moratorium on adoptions. Regardless, I was trying to eat breakfast in the adoption capital of the world and could not have felt more annoyed.

JUNE 27, 2007: NEBAJ

I get back to my house. The power has been out all day. I get a phone call from Anthony Hicks, an Appropriate Technology trainee from South Carolina.

"Hey man, have you heard the news?"

"What are you talking about, Tony?"

"It's Mike. He's out."

"Mike?"

"Yeah, the guy from Texas. He's the really skinny guy."

"He quit?"

"No, the Peace Corps administration asked him to leave. They said they just didn't think he would be a good volunteer. They said he was just too quiet and that he didn't show enough initiative. I talked to him today; he was pretty shook up."

"I would be too. Wow, that's news to me. Thanks for the update, Tony."

"Yep, talk to you later."

I later discovered that Mike was given a choice. He was told that he could either voluntarily quit or, if not, the Peace Corps administration would be forced to officially terminate him. Both bad outcomes, but he chose the former. Getting kicked out would have been a more serious résumé blemish.

The rationale behind this decision: the kid did not speak enough, and he was not active enough during training. The Peace Corps—especially my APCD, Basilio Estrada—did not think that he could properly represent the Peace Corps in a village. This shocks me, because four or five people in my training group were quiet and lazy. None of those people ever had a problem. In fact, I have never heard of this happening in any Peace Corps country anywhere.

JULY 1, 2007

The Sunday *Prensa Libre* is required reading for all expatriates living in Guatemala; it even comes with a *New York Times* supplement. Today, I read an article about "Freegans" in that very supplement. Freegans are people who are against all aspects of consumerism. They roll around in dumpsters and call it shopping. I call that lazy. They negotiate with restaurant owners for scraps of food, hoping to get free leftovers and call it pragmatic. I call that pathetic. Some people are so ridiculous. Freegans are listless bums masquerading as conscientious consumers. What a joke.

THE FOURTH OF JULY 2007 PEACE CORPS PARTY

The Peace Corps Fourth of July Party exceeded all my expectations. The party was great. The food was good, and the beers only cost 5Q. There had been contentious debate between PCVs and the Peace Corps administration on this issue. Last year, the event had been held at the Marine House in Guatemala City. PCVs boarded private camionetas that took them to the capital. The administration has decided that it would be safer to hold the event at the training center in Santa Lucía. Officially, alcohol consumption on Peace Corps property is prohibited. However, the country director can waive the rule at his or her discretion. Country Director Todd Sloan made the call: there would be beers and burgers and music, but not at the sumptuous Marine House. This may have had something to do with how last year's party ended. A year ago, Todd had just become our new country director; before that, he was the Peace Corps country director in Nicaragua for a couple of years. Most people were meeting him for the first time that day.

At last year's Fourth of July party, Todd was even busier than he thought he would be. At the Marine House, there is a nice pool that a few PCVs had been enjoying throughout the day. Toward the end of the party, a female volunteer was thrown in. This would have been quite funny if that girl had not collided head first with another chick already in the water. Todd had to drive both of them to the hospital; I doubt he was thrilled about that. I heard that one of them got forty stitches in the back of the head while the other needed ten on her forehead.

JULY 20, 2007: DINNER AND A THESIS IN NEBAJ

Tonight I am meeting master's candidate Blake Scott for dinner at El Descanso. Blake just finished his first year of graduate school at the University of Georgia. He is studying Latin American history. Blake is in Nebaj to do research for his thesis examining the role religion played during the peak of Guatemala's civil war.

Blake is a friend of B. J., my buddy from training who was put on a plane early because the Peace Corps desk jockeys in Washington are afraid to take risks. I told B. J. that I would be happy to meet with Blake. After a beer or two, the conversation got interesting.

"So, man, what's your take on the Peace Corps?"

"I'm not sure I understand the question."

"You're in the Peace Corps. What's your opinion of the organization after a year? Are you a fan?"

"Yes, sort of."

"What does that mean?"

"I am not exactly sure. It's complicated."

"Come on, man, I know I just met you. But please don't hold back on me. This isn't an interview. I am just curious about the Peace Corps. I think it's something I would have considered doing."

"You considered joining the Peace Corps?"

"Well, not really, but I think it's something I would have seriously considered if it was only a one-year commitment. Two years … two years just seemed like long a time."

"I understand what you mean, but it's a twenty-seven-month commitment for a reason. A lot of international development work revolves around merely existing. It's a slow process; you've just got to be ready when the time comes. Look, I've heard of volunteers living down here for two years and still getting very little work done. One year just isn't enough time to make an impact. It took me six months before I felt settled in Nebaj."

"But two years, Taylor, that's a long time."

"Yeah, but make sure that you aren't looking at the decision with a five-year lens, Blake. I'm planning on living for at least five or six more decades. If you look at it that way, two years isn't so long."

"Okay, so back to my question, what is your opinion about the Peace Corps?"

"All right, Blake, I have mixed feelings. The Peace Corps is basically a good idea. I know we do a lot of good work down here. However, I've met several lazy Peace Corps volunteers. Some people get disillusioned pretty early; they are content to just eek by doing the smallest amount of work. I know a guy, fairly well actually, who smokes pot all day and plays with a cat. He talks to this cat all the time. So I would say that some of the resources are wasted. The Peace Corps administration in Guatemala City does appreciate it when PCVs do good work, but they don't really condemn laziness or inefficiency. They just want volunteers who will hang out at their sites the entire time and stay under the radar."

"What do you mean by 'under the radar'?"

"The administration likes people who live inconspicuously and stay out of trouble. Another big problem: there's a huge disconnect between the Peace Corps bureaucrats in Washington and the PCVs actually living and working abroad."

"What do you mean?"

"I am saying that many times, Peace Corps paper pushers blindly enforce rules without looking at the context of the situation. They are so risk-averse because they care more about the Peace Corps public-relations campaign than completing work projects."

"That doesn't sound good."

"It's not good, Blake. It's terrible. Just consider B. J.'s situation. B. J. was probably the hardest working, most productive trainee in my group. He could have accomplished so much in two years. But B. J. had an accident and banged up his shoulder. Since he was going to be hurt for more than ninety days, the administrators in Washington told him he had to leave the country. The decision was made so quickly, I doubt they even entertained B. J.'s request to do his rehab in Guatemala City.

"Wow, I never knew all that. I knew B. J. was sent home because he hurt his shoulder. B. J. never told me about any of those specifics."

"It's ridiculous. You want another beer?"

"Sure."

JULY 2007: MID-SERVICE MEDICAL EXAM, DAY ONE

I am in the Antigua-Guatemala City area this week for my mid-service medical exam. This is something that every Peace Corps volunteer must do after they have been in country for a year. Over the next few days, I'll get a routine physical, go to the lab for blood work, visit the dentist, and provide three stool samples. The Peace Corps headquarters, dentist, and lab are all in Guatemala City, but I will be sleeping in Antigua.

I will also be tested for tuberculosis. In Guatemala, usually one or two PCVs per training group test positive each year. Getting tuberculosis would be disastrous for a couple of reasons. First, the treatment involves taking pills on a daily basis for nine months. Second and more importantly, people taking those TB pills must avoid alcohol during that time. No drinking for nine months! I'm not an alcoholic, but things could get unbearably boring in a hurry down here if I couldn't drink. Most other PCVs who drink would say the same thing. Please keep in mind that the majority of us live in indigenous villages, way out in the boonies.

My friend Eric Schroeder and I have scheduled our physicals and dental appointments on the same days. A lot of PCVs pair up for the medical exams. It's nice because otherwise boring days become more interesting. And you'll have somebody to share a room with at the Burkhardt. Then there is the matter of nightlife. If you're alone, Antigua is one of the best cities in the world to go out in—but going out is always more fun with a friend or two.

I am tired. My first day of mid-service meds is almost over. I wait patiently to see the skin doctor. I have some funky moles that need examining. I'm busier than I look because I cannot stop staring at my red TB dot. Besides, I'm nervous enough this afternoon. For the first time in several weeks, ramen noodles with red sauce are not for dinner. Is it strange that the sauce costs more than the noodles? Why would the Peace Corps office be calling me?

"Hello, Taylor?"

"Yes ..."

"Taylor, did you already go to the lab?"

"Yeah, why?"

"Taylor, you left your sample at the office."

Only now do I realize that I had completely misunderstood the directions I received earlier. No one shuttles cups of poo from the office in Zone 9 to the lab. PCVs wishing to poo in a cup at the office must then walk, poo in hand, to the lab. This way, those sages at the lab can tell us how screwed up we are. Man, am I embarrassed!

Going in a cup is supposed to be the straightforward part of mid-service meds. Furthermore, I am losing crucial red-dot-staring time with this degrading conversation. Will I be the first volunteer in history to err on the first day of stool sampling?

"Okay, Ana Luisa. Well ... sorry ... um. I'll just head back there after this meeting and then return to the lab."

"No, Taylor."

"What?"

"No. That sample is no good now. Unfortunately, they're going to need a new sample from you. They are open until six-thirty."

"Okay, thanks for letting me know. I'll figure something out."

"Okay, Taylor."

After the skin check, I dig deep, dashing to the McDonald's next to the lab. I remind myself that champions come to play every day. I remind myself that I'm still here to save the world. No fecal test, no matter how thorough, can stop me.

Two McFlurries, four cups of coffee, and an hour later, I step onto the playing field. I enter the lab with poise, chin up. I cannot let them know how awkward this is, or how painful I think the next ten to twenty minutes are going to be. Cup in hand, I gracefully enter the bathroom, ready to make history. Sans diarrhea, I will produce two stool samples in one afternoon. Then I will head back to the castle for a glorious celebration. There will be meat and cheese, drinking, dancing, and merrymaking into the wee hours of the morning. My name will forever remain in the annals of Peace Corps medical history. I will serve as an inspiration to others throughout the stool-sampling world.

I wage an epic battle in that tiny bathroom. Defying every law of gastrointestinal theory, I emerge victorious. Now I must return to the lab and apologize to Ana Luisa for my gross negligence.

"But Taylor, you were able to produce another sample this afternoon?"

"Yes."

"Wow."

Clearly impressed, she is making some sort of semi-serious bowing motion. And to think this lovely woman has yet to find out that I know how to say *thank you* in eight languages. Should I also mention that I use organic lavender hand sanitizer?

Unconquered, I head back to Antigua feeling relieved. Now I can and will spend at least eighteen of the next thirty hours staring at my red dot. I will be at the Burkhardt within an hour.

The Burkhardt is the other popular hostel for PCVs staying in Antigua. It's significantly nicer than the 58B. At 50Q a person, all rooms have a hot shower and cable television. The only downside is that all rooms are double rooms. So if you don't have a planned roommate, you're really rolling the dice. I have met tons of Peace Corps weirdoes already; I won't stay at the Burkhardt unless I have a friend to share a room with.

DAY THREE OF MID-SERVICE MEDS

I am at the Peace Corps office in Guatemala City. I restively wait to see a nurse. My red dot has not risen, which means I am TB-free! But a nurse has to check my arm to make it official. Nurse Johanna calls me into her office.

"Okay Taylor, let's have a look at that left arm."

"Sure. I think I'm clean."

"Yeah, you are."

An ocean of peace washes over me; somehow I feel that I have narrowly avoided disaster. This doesn't make much sense, but I don't feel like dwelling on my nonsensical rationalizations. I think I am totally healthy. I am wrong.

"I took a look at your lab results."

"Is everything fine?"

"We found protozoa in one of your stool samples."

"Protozoa?"

"Yes, *Blastocytis hominis.*"

"So what does that mean?"

"Well, have you been nauseated at all during these last few months? Or do you have any severe stomach pain?"

"No."

"And have you been passing out?"

"No. I probably would have mentioned that."

"All right, then you're fine. That can happen with some people, though it is rare. This protozoa is actually common in developing countries. As a policy, Peace Corps doesn't treat it unless it is adversely affecting your health, which it does not sound like it is. Eventually, you will just shed it when you move back to the US."

"I'll shed it?"

"That's right. It will eventually work its way out of your system."

"So I'm fine."

"Yes."

"And what about my weight?"

"One hundred and thirty-nine pounds."

"Yeah, that sounds really low. I usually weigh around one-fifty."

"Right, well, most guys do lose weight while they are down here. That could be for a number of reasons, primarily increased physical activity combined with healthier eating habits."

"Should I be worrying about my weight?"

"No, not unless it's bothering you. I'll e-mail you a few documents on healthy weight gain."

"Okay, sure. Thanks."

"You're very welcome. Have a safe trip back to Nebaj."

"I'll try."

I cannot believe I just had a conversation about healthy weight gain. I also cannot believe that I weigh 139 pounds. I'm nearly six feet tall. I get a call from Eric and plan to meet him at Reilly's for some happy hour beers. We are both ready for a big night in Antigua. We will be celebrating our tuberculosis-free existence. I grab a taxi to a garage in Zona 3, the spot where all the Guate-Antigua buses begin their route. I will be enjoying a hot shower before I know it.

ELEVEN: CONSOLIDATION SENSATION

JULY 24, 2007: XEMAMATZE

I'm in Xemamatze doing another water survey with Diego just outside of Nebaj. Over lunch, I listen to people talk about the war in the 1980s. I grab one last tortilla to clean my plate. Then I ask Diego what they were discussing, since I still don't know much Ixil. Diego told me that one community member was recounting a few of his most vivid memories. This guy saw a soldier cut his younger brother's hands off and then smash his head in with a rock, killing him. The man said that he isn't sure why they let him live. That's crazy. What type of person could do that to another human being?

AUGUST 22, 2007: PEACE CORPS GUATEMALA CONSOLIDATION

I just returned from a two-night Peace Corps-sanctioned sojourn in Chichicastenango. All PCVs were told to consolidate because of Hurricane Dean. Peace Corps consolidation could take place for a number of reasons—with political unrest, inclement weather, or some sort of pandemic being the most likely scenarios. Peace Corps Guatemala is acting with extreme caution this time. In 2005, Hurricane Stan ripped through the country and caused all kinds of damage. There were innumerable landslides, and many phone towers were knocked down. Peace Corps had chosen not to consolidate. As a result, they were not able to immediately confirm that all PCVs in country were safe. The administration simply could not get in touch with some people. Peace Corps Washington was breathing down their neck, not a good situation. Granted, Todd Sloan was not the Guatemala country director in 2005. However, current Peace Corps Safety and Security Coordinator Makali Bruton held the same position in 2005. There were widespread rumors that the man was nearly fired. He may have learned his lesson.

There are several consolidation points throughout the country. Most PCVs living in El Quiché are told to report to the Casa del Rey, a hotel just outside of the city. This means that most of the volunteers in my department got together, drank cheap rum, and played cards all night. Everyone took advantage of a great shower and free meals. Hurricane Dean slammed into the Yucatán Peninsula yesterday morning, causing considerable damage. The hurricane had already killed several people. With the exception of heavy rains and possibly some landslides, it looks like Guatemala will get away unscathed.

AUGUST 23, 2007

I work all day on a project proposal for Global Water, an international NGO based in California. I cannot remember the last time I worked ten hours in one day. While I am not averse to hard work, "work" in the Peace Corps is different. So much of successful development work revolves around remaining vigilant and then taking the initiative when an opportunity presents itself. In a way it's like fishing; there are certain aspects of the job that I just can't control. I've got to be ready when the time comes. Committing to live in Nebaj for an extended period and already speaking Spanish are good starts.

I lie in bed exhausted, but I cannot find sleep. There is too much noise in the street, mostly the sounds of traffic and equally annoying fireworks. Is it possible to become physically dependent upon earplugs? Before coming here, I had never used them. I now believe that Guatemala and Iraq are the two noisiest countries in the world.

SEPTEMBER 3, 2007: CONSOLIDATION #2

Tomorrow morning, Peace Corps Guatemala will consolidate yet again. Hurricane Felix is also Category Five hurricane and should be hitting Guatemala on Wednesday morning. I am not ready for another consolidation; I barely got through the last one without killing somebody. Consolidation is fun initially, but then everybody gets a little stir crazy. The booze is flowing, personalities clash, and everybody wants to head back to their sites. I want to stay in Nebaj right now and work. Plus, the Guatemalan presidential elections will be held shortly. There is a lot going on down here. Guatemala—this place is hot. I can't believe I just wrote that.

Alcohol will not be sold on the Saturday before the election or on election-day Sunday. An astute PCV must prepare accordingly. I bought two bottles of cheap rum this afternoon; one never knows when they might come in handy. I recently booked a flight to Dallas on November 2. After a year and a half in Guatemala, I will be vacationing in the United States for a week and a half. I don't know how I'll feel when my plane touches down in Dallas.

SEPTEMBER 5, 2007

Hurricane Felix is fizzling out, much like Hurricane Dean— though I am speaking strictly from a myopic Guatemalan perspective. I do not have time to worry about the rest of the world right now. This time only eight volunteers consolidated in Chichicastenango, an incredibly small number. Still, to drink Ron Botrán, play cards, listen to music, and get an update on world affairs by reading *Newsweek*, eight is plenty. Evidently, the other PCVs went to the consolidation point in Cobán. At least thirty

PCVs each are staying in Antigua and Xela. I have already heard some rowdy stories coming out of those two places.

The next morning we are released. I need to return to Nebaj. Still, I could wait until tomorrow morning. Yes, the shower at the Casa del Rey is just that good, a perfect mix of pressure and heat. Furthermore, coming down to Chichicastenango, which PCVs just call "Chichi," for only one night seems silly. I shower one more time for no reason. Then I'm out the door to catch a camioneta back to Nebaj.

SEPTEMBER 7, 2007

Lynn, Diego, Dionysio, and I meet at the Agua Para la Salud office to discuss our agenda through October. Afterward, Diego and I ride up to El Mirador to present a detailed project proposal to the community members. As always, we will be asking for them to cover 10 percent of the material costs. Plus, each beneficiary will need to have one family member work with us every day until the project is finished. We will be renovating an existing water system and building sixteen 2,000-liter ferro-cement tanks to capture rainwater. The entire project should last three months.

On the way to El Mirador, Diego and I discuss Sunday's presidential elections. I am pretty excited. Monday has been declared a national holiday. Diego tells me he's not sure who he'll vote for. The two front-runners are the center-left Álvaro Colom and the conservative General Otto Pérez Molina. Colom, an engineer, says he will reduce poverty and fight for the rights of indigenous people. General Pérez Molina says that he will crack down on crime. Pérez Molina is a heartless bastard who committed unthinkable human-rights violations during the civil war, but his message seems to be resonating with the electorate. He is leading in the polls. Security is the most important issue for most Guatemalans.

Then Diego and I discuss political advertising. I ask Diego if he knows that there is a law in this country prohibiting political campaigning before May 1. He looks at me like I'm crazy. We both know every party participating in this year's election violated that law. Advertisements were put up long before May 1. In Guatemala, this blatant disregard for the law comes as no surprise. Impunity is the law of the land down here.

I recently read an article that said only 1 percent of violent crimes are successfully prosecuted in Guatemala. That's ridiculous.

SEPTEMBER 9, 2007

Josh, Chris, and I celebrate the arrival of professional football with several *litros* of Gallo. The general and Álvaro Colom are left standing for the election's second round, since no one earned a majority.

The following morning, I learn that the corrupt FRG (Frente Republicano Guatemalteco) mayor has been reelected in Nebaj. There's talk about how this is because he buys votes in the villages. It was a very close race and a tough loss for GANA, the party of current president Oscar Berger. Guatemalans are skeptical of politicians. Yes, Americans view their own political system with a certain degree of skepticism, but in Guatemala the situation is vastly different. More than twenty political parties participated in the first round of the presidential election. After all the votes are counted, congressmen will scramble to form tenuous alliances, ideally with other parties that performed well in the election. And, of course, few congressmen are indigenous. The people have been oppressed for the last five centuries, and the oppression just continues. Poverty, malnutrition, and illiteracy were not problems before the Spanish arrived in the sixteenth century. They sure as hell are problems now.

Later that day, Diego gives me a call. He tells me that he has a joke. I say okay. Then he asks me if I know what FRG stands for. I tell him Frente Republicano Guatemalteco. Then he tells me that it actually stands for Fácil Robar Guatemala—Easy to Rob Guatemala. That is his joke. Corruption and embezzlement are key components of Guatemalan governance. Over the past twenty years, no party has taken advantage of this more than the FRG. This is the party that ruthless dictator Ríos Montt founded. Fortunately, the FRG is currently a much weaker party than it was ten years ago. Guatemalan humor is strange. When Guatemalans tell me jokes, I rarely find them funny, usually because they are too immature or simple. I'm proud of Diego for this one.

September 12, 2007

The entire Agua Para la Salud team goes up to Palop Chiquito for an inauguration. We drive for over thirty minutes and then spend an hour walking uphill to the village. I fall down six or seven times on my way up. The ground is so soggy; I don't understand how the masons can scale a mountain so adroitly. At least we have a trail to follow. Had it been raining, it might have taken me five hours to get there.

For a Westerner, witnessing an inauguration in rural Guatemala is a memorable cultural experience. An inauguration is a common yet exciting celebration in Guatemala—like celebrating a newly constructed school, a potable water system, latrines, or a hand-washing station. The entire town will gather at the school at a specific hour. In the villages, the school is usually the center of town. Always thinking of other people, Lynn likes to bring big bags of candy with him to give to the villagers.

Marimba music will be playing nonstop. Local community leaders will give speeches. These speeches are usually spoken in one of the twenty-three Mayan languages. If any foreign donors are attending the ceremony, they might say a few words. Afterward, the community usually presents the NGO and any sponsors with a small gift. Many times *morales* (Guatemalan bags) are given. The name of the town and the date are usually woven into the handmade bags. Then everyone celebrates with lunch—typically a beef or vegetable stew and steaming piles of tamales. This is a happy day for everyone involved.

Our NGO has built a set of latrines at the school. The community president gives a speech, and then Diego speaks briefly. Diego is an excellent public speaker. He decides to address the crowd in Ixil, so I only understand six words during his ten-minute discourse. When Diego finishes, he and Lynn are each given a *moral*. In expatriate American parlance, a moral is known as man purse. Lynn's probably been given at least fifty of those colorful handmade things over the past decade and a half. He probably has the greatest Guatemalan moral collection of any gringo in the history of Guatemalan moral collection by gringos.

After that, Lynn is asked to say a few words. I think he is a bit surprised by the request. I'm also surprised. I've been to several inaugurations with Lynn, but he is seldom asked to speak formally. Lynn learned all his Spanish in his fifties. Having said that, he speaks fluently; he just has a horrendous accent, which isn't an issue since everyone is able to understand him. Always quick and to the point, today Lynn Roberts rocks the house.

"Bueno, gracias a todos por todo su apoyo con este proyecto. Creo que todo estamos muy felices por tener nuevas letrinas en la escuela para el beneficio de los niños. Siempre estoy pensando en hacer más proyectos aquí en Palop Chiquito. De hecho, espero regresar a Palop Chiquito pronto. Y cuando regrese, voy a regresar con una moral llena de dinero para realizar más proyectos."

"Well, I want to thank everyone for all of their support with this Project. I think we are all very happy about the new latrines in the school. I am always thinking of doing more projects here in Palop Chiquito. In fact, I hope to return to Palop Chiquito soon. And when I do, I am going to return with a sack full of money to carry out more projects."

Again, I have seen Lynn speak publicly on many occasions, but this was his best performance. He returns to his seat with rousing applause. Lynn Roberts is a mythical figure in the Ixil Triangle. Since 1994, I doubt that anybody has completed more projects in the area than he has. He's the godfather of development work up here.

Beef stew and tamales are always served. I notice that some men are even stuffing tamales into their jacket pockets as they leave. I don't know why this has caught me off guard. These people are unbelievably poor.

MY AUSTRIAN AMIGA

That weekend in Antigua, I hook up with a girl named Karina from Austria. She is gorgeous. Normally I'm not attracted to girls with short hair, but I don't have a problem flirting with her. She might be the most aggressive girl I've ever been with. She initiates everything, and I let it all happen. I am drinking my second Heineken at Riki's when she approaches me at the bar. My plan is to have a couple beers there and then meet up with a bunch of Peace Corps friends at Mono Loco around ten-thirty. Initially, she tries to ask me something in Spanish, but her language skills leave something to be desired. I adjust accordingly.

"Do you speak English?"

"Yes."

"Where are you from?"

"Austria."

"Austria. I love Austria."

"You've been to Austria? What were you doing there?"

"I studied there. I took summer classes at the University of Innsbruck."

"American, right?"

"Yeah."

"I've been traveling in Mexico and Guatemala for over a month. You are the first person I've met who has been to Austria."

"It's a beautiful country. I love Europe."

"And how long have you been in Guatemala?"

"A little more than a year."

"You live in Antigua?"

"No, I live in a town called Nebaj. It's about six hours north of here."

"And what are you doing in Nebaj?"

"I design water systems, really basic engineering."

"Do you like it?"

"Yeah, it's cool. Your English is great."

"Thanks. Everyone in Austria speaks English. We start learning when we're young."

"Oh, right. I guess I had forgotten about that. Most Europeans speak at least two languages."

"And you Americans only speak English. And you guys never travel."

"Not all of us. I've been down here a lot longer than you have. Remember?"

"My name's Karina."

"I'm Taylor."

"Nice to meet you, Taylor."

"Likewise. Listen, Karina, I'm about to go meet up with some other friends at another bar. Would you be interested in going over there?"

"Sure, but where?"

"It's called Mono Loco. It's a short walk from here."

"When are we leaving?"

"Right after you finish your beer."

Karina and I meet up with Eric, J. P., and several other Peace Corps volunteers. After Mono Loco, we go to Red's to shoot some pool. Karina is traveling alone, so she is happy to join us. I haven't been with a woman in over a year, so I am delighted to have her join us. The next morning, I wake up with a vicious hangover. I have just slept with a girl I had met only hours before. This is something that I would've never done back home.

"Taylor, what are you doing today?"

"Watching college football."

"All day?"

"Yeah, I think so. There will be games all day."

"Oh, would you be interested in climbing Pacaya?"

"Are you kidding? With this hangover, no way."

"Okay. I'd like to, though. Since this is my last day in Antigua."

"Sorry lady, you're welcome to join me at Mono Loco for football, but that's as active as I plan on being today." (I should add that I frequently address girls my age as "lady" when I am speaking directly to them.)

I decide to walk Karina to the hotel lobby. She still looks beautiful in spite of our evening of excess.

"All right, Karina. Adiós. Fue un placer."

"Yeah, see you in the next life."

I give her a kiss on the cheek and point her in the direction of her hostel. Gingerly, I walk back to my room for a shower. The games are starting soon, and I need to pick up the pace.

TWELVE: HIGHWAY ROBBERY

SEPTEMBER 23, 2007

I'm watching the second half of the Georgia-Alabama game on the Internet at El Descanso. The Dawgs win 26-23 in overtime. I use the term "watch" loosely. I never actually see the game. I paid for four hours of Internet access and refreshed ESPN GameCast to follow the action. I order a 13Q beer at the restaurant bar and then bring it into the computer room. I will repeat this process at least five times over the course of a football game. This may sound pathetic, but for a true sports fan, it's better than nothing. Clearly, it would have been more fun in Tuscaloosa, standing with my fraternity brothers, secretly mixing bourbon drinks in the stands. But SEC football, my college buddies, and Maker's Mark are not going anywhere. I need to finish what I started in Guatemala.

I walk back home alone and see a drunken brawl in the street with two indigenous men screaming at each other in Ixil. Some Ixils go nuts when they get too much of that firewater in them.

I get back to my house, brush my teeth, and decide to read a *Prensa Libre* that I bought a few days ago. There's a small reference to Latin American immigration in the business section. I start thinking: if I were Guatemalan and had little formal education, would I attempt to work in the United States illegally? Of course I would, because that makes sense. I have had Ixils tell me that they earned anywhere from eighty-five to one hundred forty dollars a day in the United States. These were guys who had worked on construction sites. These men would be lucky if they earned ten dollars a day working construction in Guatemala, especially if they aren't in Guatemala City or Xela. Most Guatemalans make nowhere near that kind of money.

Immigration is a highly contentious subject in the United States, largely because it arouses many contradictory feelings. For example, the United States is a nation of immigrants, so we should be accepting of people who have migrated recently. But the United States must also enforce the laws we have put in place. Yet we want the cheap labor; immigrants fill employment gaps. Immigrants take jobs that Americans aren't willing to take. Or no, immigrants take jobs at wages that Americans deem unacceptable. Perhaps we should get rid of all immigrants before they bankrupt our health-care system. Several hospitals in Arizona have already been shut down. Maybe these immigrants have just as much of a right to be in the United States as I do. Yep, immigration is an issue with no easy solution. So far, policymakers have been too scared to act because they don't want to scare off any potential voters. I just hope that our government doesn't decide to do something idiotic like build a wall across our southern border. That would be a sad day in United States history.

SEPTEMBER 25, 2007

I hold my fifth meeting in El Mirador today. I am trying to do a project there to renovate the existing water system and build a few dozen ferro-cement tanks to capture rainwater. I have been working on this project for a couple of months; the people of El Mirador are not easy to work with. We finally agree on a budget and a timetable. The contentious issue today is inclement weather. Actually, the contentious issue today is the possibility of inclement weather. Again, the weather in the Ixil Triangle is an aberration. Aside from parts of the country that have been officially designated as tropical rainforests, this area is the wettest part of the nation. I have never seen rain like this before. If rain could be compared to cars, then Seattle rain might be a four-door Chevy Tahoe, but Nebaj rain would be a Hummer.

This is great for vegetation, but can impede the flow of development projects. Excessive rainfall worsens road conditions, which are already horrible. What is more, it triggers landslides—blocking roads entirely, destroying homes, even killing people. For all of our projects, we hire a *camión* (large truck) to deliver the heaviest materials to the remote villages before the project begins. When roads are really muddy, two things can happen. One, a truck may be able to deliver the supplies but then get stuck on the way back because of the lightened load. Or two, the road might be so bad that the truck can't make it all the way to the village. In which case, villagers would have to carry a hell of a lot of sand, gravel, and cement to their town. This is backbreaking, time-consuming manual labor of the worst kind.

The committee members of El Mirador, the village's leaders, don't think the road is passable. They want to delay the project until the spring, when road conditions improve.

I am now even more frustrated with this project, although the people of El Mirador do have a point. I wouldn't want to carry all of those materials from the *cruce* in Vicalamá all the way to El Mirador. We will make a final decision next week. If the road's not passable by then, we'll postpone the project until April.

SEPTEMBER 29, 2007

Presidential candidate General Otto Pérez Molina is holding a rally in Nebaj. That guy must have an enormous pair of cojones. For well over a year during the civil war, Pérez Molina ran the G-2, military intelligence. In other words, he had a hand in the deaths of thousands in Ixil country, one of the key areas of conflict during that time. Even more appalling is that the man's campaign slogan is "Mano Dura." This basically means "Iron First" or "Firm Hand." The general is making a statement. He will crack down on crime if he is elected. But really, if he were president, he would have little to do with this. Furthermore, during the civil war, applying "mano dura" meant, literally, assassinating a guerrilla fighter. Everyone is aware of this, and yet he still has widespread support throughout the country. As far as Guatemalan elections go, it usually is a question of picking the lesser of two evils. Álvaro Colom is no saint, but I hope he wins the presidency.

LATIN AMERICAN IDOL

Latin American Idol winner Carlos Peña is the talk of the entire country. Guatemalans feel so inferior to Mexicans. The finals were that much more intense since Peña competed against a Mexican. And he won! This was front-page news across the country and the lead story on any reputable TV program. Shortly thereafter, I noticed a Carlos Peña TV commercial, congratulating him on his victory. There was small writing at the bottom of the screen. At first I thought I'd misread something. But no: the ads were paid for by the Guatemalan government. That's terrific. Nice use of funds. Guatemala, when will you learn? This country has so many problems. Peña's life has been a cakewalk compared to most of the country where people are mired in poverty and illiteracy. Where I live, people don't have enough to eat! Someone stop this madness.

OCTOBER 9, 2007: RURAL HEALTH

Diego and I are doing health surveys in Xecoxo all day. We gather information about family size, eating habits, food security, and other issues related to health and hygiene. I have still not gotten used to hearing roosters crow all day. And those roosters definitely don't need to be lounging on people's beds. At least I have grown accustomed to hearing dogs bark incessantly. Guatemala has a countrywide canine problem; the dog population here is spinning out of control. For that matter, so is the human population. Birth control still remains a taboo subject in the western highlands. The Catholic Church has only made the situation worse. Condom use and birth control should be encouraged. When poor people have children, the situation only becomes worse. People dig themselves into a deeper hole. Land inheritances get smaller and smaller. The poor get poorer.

During my first week in Nebaj, I saw more stray dogs than I had ever seen in my entire life. Stray dogs are barking outside my house, stray dogs are barking as I walk to work in the morning, stray dogs are barking at the gas station, stray dogs are barking at the market, stray dogs are barking outside the police station, stray dogs are barking near the pool hall, stray dogs are barking at the entrance to Comedor Lupita, stray dogs are barking at the bus terminal, stray dogs are barking at Don's, stray dogs are barking outside El Descanso, stray dogs are barking by the cantina, stray dogs are barking next to Chris's house, stray dogs are barking at the central plaza as I try to read *La Prensa Libre*. Stray dogs, otherwise known as *chuchos*, have not stopped barking since I got to Nebaj.

The typical household in rural Guatemala is a germophobe's worst nightmare. Typically the houses are made of wood and poorly insulated. The dirt floors allow for germs to be transmitted easily among family members. Diego and I often see chickens and rabbits running around inside the houses. Most families cook using smoky wood fires with zero ventilation. As a result, respiratory illness is a serious problem in Guatemala.

Consequently, people frequently lie to us during the surveys, as if Diego and I work for some sort of ruthless health police— traveling to the villages to enforce proper hygiene practices at any cost. But Diego is such a good communicator, especially with Ixils, that he is usually able to find out what we need to know. He could be mayor someday, seriously.

Frequently, villages do not have access to clean drinking water. Women are forced to carry ten-liter *tinajas*, or plastic containers, on their heads to and from isolated spring sites. When Agua Para la Salud builds a water system, we take the total population of the village into consideration. We normally give villages, if possible, eighty liters of water per person per day. In the villages of Guatemala, the growth rate is approximately 3 percent. This means the population will double in twenty years. The water systems we build are designed to give a village an adequate water supply for at least two decades and sometimes much longer.

Latrines are another issue. Sometimes the word *latrina* loosely translates to "hole in the ground where people happen to use the bathroom." Other times, villagers might have nice latrines as a result of some development project. These nice latrines would be built of cement block. They would probably have cement seats and metal doors. In the Nebaj area, these nicely made latrines probably would have been built by Agua Para la Salud or Intervida, a Spanish NGO.

THE PEACE CORPS UNDERACHIEVERS
Not all Peace Corps volunteers are lively, smart, tough, or hardworking. Some are lazy. Some are complete stoners. Some are just natural sluggards who don't need weed to waste entire workweeks without even realizing it.

I know one PCV who I think is the laziest development worker in Central America. I am surprised the guy was even able to fill out all the paperwork to have his Peace Corps application processed. After two years of service, he will have built approximately thirty *estufas mejoradas*. These are the brick stoves that burn wood efficiently and channel smoke outside the house. One can be built for about 700Q or $100. Building one of these simple stoves takes eight or ten hours, split into two days. Thus, upon completion of his service, I know a guy who will have a little more than two weeks' worth of work to show for his two years in Guatemala. All he does is talk to a cat and smoke dope all day. This is so appalling I need not elaborate.

Like I said before, this guy is not alone. I have met several PCVs who are more concerned with *being* Peace Corps volunteers than with *doing* any work. These pathetic and frighteningly unimpressive people will return to the United States and brag about their Peace Corps adventures. Most of them are probably washing dishes in a New Mexico diner right now, telling themselves that they are unique, that they never bow to conformity. But their colleagues know the truth. These bums know who they are, and they should be ashamed of themselves. To clarify, I would say less than 10 percent of the PCVs I have met in Guatemala are worthless bums. The vast majority of those I met were interesting, intelligent people who did give a damn about getting things done.

OCTOBER 15, 2007

I have learned that the *cruce* is a mess, so the El Mirador project will be postponed until April. A year ago, this might have surprised me, but not now. I feel depressed and frustrated. But above all else, I am lonely. Solitude has crept up on me. I yearn for the touch of a woman.

I think I have a crush on one of the girls working at El Descanso, Rosa. She is quite cute, and I think she's single. Plus, she's at least eighteen, so everything would be legal. However, Rosa is an evangelical. This means that her parents are unreasonably strict. She has an 8:00 p.m. curfew. She doesn't go out. She isn't allowed. I doubt that she's ever taken a sip of alcohol or smoked a cigarette. Furthermore, she is a virgin. It is quite possible that she has never even made out with a guy. Yes, a fling with Rosa is getting increasingly complicated.

During the civil war, the military pilloried the Catholic Church, largely because of the Church's associations with "Liberation Theology." Highly influential in Latin America during the 1970s and 1980s, Liberation Theology has as two of its core principles the eradication of poverty and an end to political oppression. It also claims that unbridled capitalism has exploited the poor. Liberation Theology has been associated with Marxism and far-left extremists for decades. Advocates usually encourage political activism as a means for creating changes in society, both social and political.

In contrast, the Protestant church somehow managed to project an image of political neutrality during Guatemala's civil war. Because of this, Protestantism has exploded in Guatemala over the past thirty years. In the Ixil Triangle, Evangelicals (Protestants) usually live much more ascetic lives. Many of them do not drink or smoke. In some families, dancing and modern music are also forbidden.

OCTOBER 17, 2007

I'm rechecking the distribution line in Kalompatzom with Diego today. We will start putting in a water system there soon. We were just making sure we had bought enough galvanized pipe.

I think I have fallen down about sixty times today. Conversely, the Guatemalans never fall. And they are typically moving much more quickly than I am. If navigating rough terrain in uncomfortable rubber boots were an Olympic sport, Guatemala would have already won at least two dozen gold medals.

That evening, I stop by El Descanso to use the Internet. When I am finished, I tell Chico, the guy working the counter, that I want to start teaching English classes. I tell him that the class could meet two or three times a week at the Agua Para la Salud office. We have a huge blackboard and plenty of tables and chairs there. I also ask him to tell the other El Descanso employees: Jorge, Diego, Gaspar, Ricardo, and the lovely Rosa. I tell him that I would like to start as soon as possible. I tell him that I will stop by in a few days to see how many people are interested. I tell him they would be welcome to bring any friends or family members who would like to learn English.

It's sad when people only know one language. I imagine most of them do not know what they are missing. I wish I spoke six languages fluently. My knowledge of Spanish has allowed me to do some incredible things and meet some fascinating people. I wouldn't have had that kind of access if I didn't speak Spanish moderately well. It's almost as if I've discovered an entirely different world. Without Spanish skills, I would've never found a "friend" to teach me the basics of the tango in Buenos Aires. I wouldn't have been able to speak with the children at the orphanage in Mindo, Ecuador. I wouldn't have found my way back to the hotel in Puerto Vallarta. I wouldn't have gotten to know Nieves so well in Spain; we still trade e-mails from time to time. I wouldn't have been able to participate in all those discussions about American foreign policy. I wouldn't have been able to talk myself out of a few tight spots. I wouldn't have been able to examine Neruda or Bécquer in the language in which they were meant to be read. I wouldn't have been able to buy gas or get a cup of coffee in most places in Miami during my summer internship. I could go on forever, though I won't. Most importantly, I wouldn't have been able to learn as much about different people and foreign cultures. And I wouldn't have been able to learn as much about myself either. Stated simply, learning Spanish has changed my life forever.

OCTOBER 20, 2007

Today I am translating for American missionaries in San Juan de Cotzal. Cotzal is the second biggest town in Ixil country. The indigenous dress and use of the Ixil language are slightly different compared to Nebaj. However, culturally speaking, I am still in Ixil country.

That night, I sleep in Cotzal with one of our masons, Antonio Cavinal. Antonio is the proud father of eight children. His oldest son, Juan, also works at Agua Para la Salud as a mason. He's twenty-three, which means that Antonio fathered his first child when he was eighteen. That night, Antonio shares with me a precious story, that of his youngest son, Lynn. I should preface this by saying that the infant mortality rate in rural Guatemala is among the highest in the world.

It seems Antonio's wife was having trouble with her eighth pregnancy, and she had fallen gravely ill. The hospital in Nebaj, though useful, is not modern enough to deal with serious health complications. Antonio didn't know what to do, so he asked Lynn for his advice. Lynn said that Antonio should take her down to Guatemala City to have the child. The only problem with this: Antonio couldn't afford it. Most of the Agua Para la Salud masons, though well paid, live from month to month. Disposable income is hard to come by if eight children are in the picture.

Lynn agreed to loan Antonio several thousand quetzales to cover his wife's medical expenses. The baby was born without any problems. Antonio and his wife happily returned to Cotzal with their newborn child. One could logically conclude that Lynn saved the life of Antonio's wife and his newborn child.

A couple days later, Antonio came by Lynn's house to discuss repayment of his loan. The amount was so large that Antonio would need to pay Lynn back in several monthly installments. Lynn's response was, "Antonio, don't worry about it. The most important thing is that your wife is healthy and that you've brought another beautiful child into the world." He just told Antonio to keep working as hard as he had been; Antonio was a highly valued worker on any job site, and Lynn new it. It was then that Antonio realized there was only one appropriate name for his miracle baby: Lynn.

Antonio recounts this story over eggs, black beans, two stacks of steaming tortillas, and chamomile tea. We are enjoying a typical dinner at his house after a hard day's work. Tears swell in my eyes. I try to conceal them, but it is no use. Undoubtedly, little Lynn Cavinal will have to explain his unique, unmistakably gringo-sounding name on dozens of occasions over the course of his life. He may even get teased about it growing up, though it won't matter. He's got one hell of a story.

OCTOBER 30, 2007

This morning, I take the GRE in Guatemala City. I will be applying to master's programs at several schools this fall. I want to focus on economic or political development, an idea I would have never considered if did not join the Peace Corps. Georgetown,

Johns Hopkins, and Columbia are my top choices, because those are the best schools for what I want to study.

I am really pleased with the results. This is especially important for me, since my GPA in college was so lousy. Getting into the schools I just mentioned still won't be easy, but at least I have a chance.

I am now in a camioneta heading back to Antigua; the driver is blasting Ricardo Arjona, Guatemala's most famous musician. I will be back just in time for lunch. I am happily staring out the window when suddenly I hear screaming coming from the front.

"Teléfonos, teléfonos. Damas y caballeros, denos sus celulares por favor."

I see three men behaving erratically at the front of the camioneta. Two are holding handguns. The young men look edgy and insecure, like they are strung out on coke or methamphetamines. These guys are going to turn around and sell the phones for drug money. Since I am in the capital, I keep my cell phone in my sock when I am not using it. I quickly decide that I'm not going to give it up. This is an ill-advised, yet practical decision. If my cell phone gets stolen, I will need to buy a new one. This means that I will need to report this incident to the Peace Corps Safety and Security Coordinator. I'm already so tired of the Peace Corps bureaucracy; I will attempt to avoid it at all costs. On the other hand, if the thieves discover that I have been holding out on them, I will have far greater problems on my hands.

I look straight ahead as the men with guns race down the aisle. They probably collect fifteen or twenty phones. It all happens so fast. I am surprised that they do not ask for our wallets. I also keep that in my sock when I'm in the capital, or I wear an unnoticeable money belt inside my pants. I doubt I would have handed that over, either. I think I would have been more scared if the thieves had stayed on the camioneta longer. After the thieves leave, everyone acts as if there has been no robbery. The *ayudante* turns the music up again. Most of passengers are chatting calmly. Armed robbery is not exactly an infrequent occurrence in Guatemala City.

That night, I ride with Lynn to the Guatemala City airport. We are picking up a new volunteer, Peter Cruddas from London. Peter will be working with Agua Para la Salud for one year. He already has a master's degree in civil engineering and has lived in Botswana for a year as a development worker. Peter currently dates a girl from Zaragoza, Spain, though he says he doesn't have much in the way of language skills. We have dinner at Riki's that evening.

"So is there a good local beer?"

"Gallo is the main one. It's okay, not great. I'm sick of it. Gallo will give you an awful hangover. I usually drink Brahva now; it's from Brazil. Here in Antigua, you can get Heineken or Beck's, but they're too expensive."

"Interesting. How is it working with Lynn?"

"Lynn is awesome. He oversees most of the work at the NGO, and he has a lot of sage advice to share. He's been living down here since the mid-nineties. But Lynn does more than that. This past year, he's been more of a paternal figure than a boss or supervisor. He will look out for you while you're down here. It takes a little while to feel comfortable with him; he can be difficult to read. Just wait until you hear the masons talk about the guy. It's as if 'Lynn' were an official religion. They love the man."

"That's good to know. And how is Nebaj?"

"Peter, I love the place. There are probably fifteen to twenty thousand people there. It's small enough so you'll be able to get close to some of the locals. But at the same time, there is a certain degree of anonymity in Nebaj. Not everyone will know your name. You aren't the only Westerner in town. That area was hit so badly during the war, there is now a solid international development presence in the Ixil Triangle, mostly Spanish and American NGOs. I know the EU has recently done work up there as well."

"Do you have friends in Nebaj?"

"Yeah, sure, a couple other Peace Corps volunteers live in Nebaj. There are also a couple who live nearby, in Cotzal and Acul. We have fun up there, I promise."

"Nice, man, I'm looking forward to it. And you, you're heading back to the States I hear?"

"Yeah, for about ten days. So I'll catch up with you in a couple of weeks."

"Sounds good. How do you say *bill* in Spanish?"

"La cuenta."

"You want to ask for la cuenta?"

"Sure."

PART III

THIRTEEN: A RETURN TO THE MOTHERLAND

NOVEMBER 12, 2007

I have waited eighteen months to go home. I did this because I didn't want to confuse myself. I live and work in Guatemala; Guatemala has become my home. The more the United States feels like home, the less productive and happy I am as a PCV in Guatemala. Not surprisingly, returning to the United States feels like I am easing into a warm bath, the super-girly kind with aromatic lavender bubbles.

Dallas, my hometown, seems so huge. Everything is so clean. Upon arrival at DFW International, I want to stop at every water fountain and enjoy the cold, clean tap water. I get bloated after about five stops. My dad picks me up from the airport. We hug. He looks younger. I give my mom a big hug when I get back to the house. Then she starts crying. The three of us talk for about an hour. After that, I meander through the house for a few minutes. The place seems inordinately clean. There is so much order here. It smells pleasant. The floors are made of wood, not dirt. I see a huge refrigerator. And there's a ton of food inside! I had forgotten that there are so many different options in the United States— restaurants, museums, beers, newspapers, movie theaters, cable

TV channels, magazines, cars, computers. The possibilities here seem endless.

I enter my bedroom upstairs, and it feels like I have just checked into a four-star hotel. I cannot believe it. I grew up in this house. How could I have forgotten how nice it was? I am in paradise. Maybe I didn't forget anything. Maybe I just took certain things for granted. Maybe I just took everything for granted. Reality has not changed; my perceptions have changed. My experiences in Guatemala have changed me.

After a few days in Dallas, I travel to my alma mater for the Georgia-Auburn game. Outside Sanford Stadium, my friend Alex and I get a great deal on a pair of tickets.

"Hey man, what are those going for?"

"I got two for one-sixty. What do y'all say?"

"A hundred and sixty dollars? We can't do that. No way."

Alex and I keep walking. Then an idea hits me. I walk back to find the last guy we were talking to.

"Hey man."

"What up?"

"You still got those two for one-sixty? How about I give you a hundred and we call it even."

"Man, are you crazy? These seats are lower level. This is Georgia-Auburn. What makes you think you're special?"

"Nothing. Listen, man, help me out. I graduated from UGA in 2005. I've been living in Guatemala for the last eighteen months. I'm a Peace Corps volunteer, and this is the first time I've been back to the US. I'm on a really tight budget, so what do you say?"

"Peace Corps? Are you for real man?"

"You think I just made that up? Nobody's that clever."

"Peace Corps. I'm actually thinking of applying. I'd like to go to Africa. Two years is a long time, though. Can I request Africa on my application? Do you know?"

"Yeah, Africa is one of the regions you can pick. So you could list Africa as your regional preference. They don't let you pick individual countries, though."

"That's interesting."

"So what do you say about those tickets? I still got a hundred bucks."

"You know what? Just give me eighty. I'll give you the Peace Corps discount."

"Sweet. Thanks man."

"It's a pleasure. Enjoy the game."

"You too, buddy."

"When do you go back?"

"Next Tuesday."

"Stay safe down there, all right?"

"I'll do my best. But first we've got to pull these Dawgs through."

"You're right about that."

Georgia kills Auburn, 45–20. I am in heaven. I get to see most of my close friends from college. I eat some terrific food—hash browns, grits, a chili cheeseburger, tasty beer, pizza, walnut brownies, squash casserole, cornbread, mashed potatoes, a calzone, and more. I am glad that I haven't forgotten how to feed myself properly. This comes as a relief.

I had also forgotten how fun college was. That Saturday, I drank outstanding beer on North Campus and mingled with hundreds of my former classmates. Most of the girls were quite attractive. Almost all of them wore classy black dresses. And these girls are usually in favor of lowering taxes! I was in heaven. In some ways, it felt like I'd never left college. It was that easy to slide back into the rhythm of undergraduate life. I didn't want that Saturday to end. The only frustrating part of my trip home: at times, I was unable to remember certain words in English. I had forgotten how to say words like "hubcap," "coaster," "blender," and "stapler." Dauntlessly, I used my fluent English to manage those challenges appropriately.

NOVEMBER 13, 2007

My American sojourn is over. I'm back at the 58B in Antigua. I will spend the next couple of nights in Antigua, reading, walking, visiting art galleries, browsing in used bookstores, and drinking a lot of coffee from Café Condessa, my favorite spot for coffee in the country. I usually order a *cortadito* and then immediately reenter the line to get another one. It may not make much sense, but it has become my ritual. Before I know it, I will be back in Nebaj.

Most Peace Corps volunteers buffer a trip to the United States with a few days in Antigua. Going straight back to one's site would be tough, unless I were one of the three PCVs who currently live within walking distance from Antigua's central park. I can't believe that PCVs are even allowed to live around here; everything is so nice. I am surprised that I don't have more to say. I cannot find the appropriate words. I am too tired for reflection and too confused for introspection.

Fourteen: Army Ranger

*"Our body is a machine for living. It is organized for
that, it is its nature. Let life go on in it unhindered
and let it defend itself."*

—*Leo Tolstoy*

November 2007

I'm at Mono Loco for a day of college football. I am relaxed and
ready to fill my afternoon with pigskin and cold beer.

At the bar, some guy named Albo is buying everybody tequila
shots. It's eleven in the morning. I'm not even ready for a beer. He
winds up sitting next to me, so we start talking. This guy has done
three tours in Iraq as an Army Ranger. He thinks he's killed about
thirty people. He has been shot twice and has the scars to prove it.
He gratuitously lifts up his shirt to make sure I believe him. Albo
tells me that he likes drinking. He tells me that since he returned
from his third tour, he has wanted to stay drunk. He tells me he's
an alcoholic. He tells me he's thought about killing himself. I
just met this guy five minutes ago. Our entire conversation seems
surreal and distant, as if it were not really happening. Albo hasn't
finished.

"You know the worst? What did you say your name was, man?"

"Taylor. My name's Taylor."

"You know the worst part about all that shit in Iraq?"

"No man, I don't."

"I killed all those people. I killed all those people, and I'm not sure that they needed to die. I was a killing machine over there. I don't know how I did it. Three tours, Tyler. Did I tell you I did three tours over there in Iraq, Tyler?"

"You may have mentioned it, Albo."

"Well, that shit's fucked up."

"I hear you man; I'm gonna hit the head. I'll catch up with you later, all right."

"Peace, man."

Obviously I don't need to use the bathroom, but it is the only escape tactic I can come up with. The bathroom in the Mono Loco is tiny. I decide to use a stall and just sit on the toilet seat in case Albo follows me in. I sit patiently for five or ten minutes and send a few text messages to other PCVs who are in Antigua this weekend. When I return to my seat at the bar, Albo has moved on and is talking to a young Guatemalan couple at one of the tables near the entrance. I know Albo is hurting, and I feel for the guy. Unfortunately, there is nothing I can do to help him. The human costs of war are so great. I learned this long before I met Albo. My paternal grandfather was killed in Vietnam in 1965. He left behind a lovely wife and five boys. Albo is one of many. Will the senseless killing ever stop?

DECEMBER 2, 2007

My new colleague Peter and I get along quite well. It's great to have another Westerner at the office, for so many reasons. Now I can use Peter as a sounding board and vice versa. I have more flexibility with regards to scheduling; since we have two water engineers at the office, I will not be required to lead all of the water surveys. Furthermore, it's way more fun and entertaining to have a native English speaker around. Lynn is intricately involved in all of the projects, but he is more of a supervisor, fund-raiser, and money manager. Peter and I are the ones who'll be out there mixing it up in the villages on a regular basis. We'll write the formal project proposals, and we're responsible for water-system design at the office. While Lynn knows how to do all this, his efforts are better spent elsewhere. I should add that Lynn is tireless. The man is unbelievably productive. He has more energy than I do. Though he's in his mid-sixties, he looks at least ten years younger.

December 3, 2007

I am translating at the local hospital in Nebaj; I will surely see some depressing stuff. Partners for Surgery, a Virginia-based nonprofit, will conduct a medical mission in Guatemala this week. Partners for Surgery tries to give rural community members access to surgical procedures. They also strive to educate Guatemalans about important health and hygiene practices. This time, most of the doctors are from Canada. I would have eventually found that out after working with them for a couple hours, but that won't be necessary. As soon as they get to the hospital, before they even take out any medical supplies, two of them start to put up Canadian flags everywhere. Interesting.

Partners for Surgery works with a Guatemalan NGO, Compañeros en Salud, while in Guatemala. I am assigned to work with Dr. John. The Ixil translator's name is Ricardo. Ricardo has worked at El Descanso for years and is a good guy. I see all sorts of physiological anomalies today, but the most disturbing is a little boy with a tail about four inches long. Dr. John likes to take pictures for his records. Of course, he snaps a few of that tail. Afterward, he tells me that the "irregular growth" is probably due to malnutrition, and it could be removed easily. Mainly, we see cleft palates and hernias.

Yesterday, I told Diego that I would be working as a translator for a medical mission. I told him to give me a call if he had a problem or question at our office. Then Diego told me that his oldest daughter has a vaginal problem. I encouraged them to drop by the hospital at the end of the day.

At around four o'clock, Diego's wife, Catarina, arrives at the hospital with her eldest daughter. Dr. John and I have been working exclusively with male patients throughout the day. Another doctor, Kathy, has been working with the females. However, our orderly system changes late in the afternoon. In an effort to work everyone in, we no longer have two separate lines, but one larger one. Diego's daughter is assigned to Dr. John's room. I greet her as she and her mother enter. I then explain her situation to John. In order to avoid any embarrassment for them or me, I leave right after that. Diego's daughter picks up her prescription fifteen minutes later. I see them at the medical counter and walk over to say good-bye. Catarina is holding the pills and then whispers to me for clarification.

"Taylor? ¿Están seguros sobre esto? Ellos son expertos, ¿verdad?"

"Sí, todo va a salir bien. Ellos tienen mucho conocimiento."

"Pero, adentro, verdad, ¿de verdad eso es necesario?"

"Taylor? Are are the doctors sure about this? They are experts, right?"

"Yes, everything will be fine. They are very knowledgeable."

"But inside, that's really necessary?"

And then it hits me. Catarina has misunderstood. Yes, her daughter is to take pills, but the conventional way, orally. She does not need to insert pills into her vagina. Thank God she asked! At times, I felt like crying today, but I restrained myself. At the very least, my time in Guatemala has taught me a great deal about the human psyche. Sometimes, unwittingly, I have been able to probe deeply into the consciousness of others, figuring out what makes them tick. However, my introspective examination has been far more profound. People are struggling with the pernicious effects of poverty and illiteracy on a daily basis. All over the world, around three billion people live on less than two dollars a day. In comparison, my life has been a walk in the park. I don't have a right to complain about anything ever again. Receding hairlines, awkward dates, and car troubles are the penthouse suite of personal complaints. Billions of people would love to face my trivial troubles. For most of the world, it would probably feel like a day spent at an amusement park. My life is so easy. My only regret is that it took me more than twenty-three years to figure this out.

Also today, I see a young girl with an expanded stomach. She couldn't weigh more than thirty pounds, but her stomach is enormous. It looks like the little girl had swallowed a fully inflated volleyball. And she couldn't be more than seven or eight years old. The doctor says there's probably a grave problem with her spleen, most likely a tumor. All the doctors seem to be in agreement: this little girl has cancer. She'll die within a few months, a year at the most, if she doesn't get some serious help. The words "serious help" in Guatemalan medical parlance can be roughly translated to "get your ass down to the capital for a more thorough medical examination." Her mother is told this, but she refuses to heed the doctor's advice and go to Guatemala City. Why? Mom is afraid of the chicken buses. She doesn't like Guatemala City. It's too big, and she feels uncomfortable there.

"Pero, señora, tienen que ir."

"Hablamos de tu hijita. Podría ser cuestión de vida o muerte."

"Vaya, pero tengo miedo. No, no vamos en camioneta para Guate. No quiero discutirlo más."

"But ma'am, you all have to go."

"We are talking about your little girl. It could be a question of life or death."

"Okay, but I'm scared. No, we are not going to take a bus to Guatemala City. I don't want to discuss this any more."

The mother's Spanish is surprisingly good. Most older women in the Ixil Triangle do not speak any Spanish. Nevertheless, I still cannot believe what just transpired. Is she really that terrified of Guatemala City? Could I be missing something? My own mother would accompany me to the moon to prolong my life for even a few additional days. And she doesn't even like to fly. I left the hospital with a bitter taste in my mouth that afternoon. How could a culture breed such irrational phobias?

I head to El Descanso to use the Internet after translating. My heart flutters with youthful anticipation. Dear Rosa has told me she will be working tomorrow at the health center in Salquil Grande—the site of tomorrow's medical mission. We will be working together. I feel like I've won the lottery. The following morning, I am crushed to discover that Rosa will not be coming after all.

DECEMBER 9, 2007: MY TWENTY-FIFTH BIRTHDAY

About fifteen of us are in Antigua to celebrate my birthday. We eat dinner at Café No Se, which means "Café I Don't Know" in English. After that, we go to Sky Bar for a couple drinks. Sky Bar has the best view in Antigua; from the rooftop bar, we are able to see the three large volcanoes that surround the city—Agua, Acatenango, and Fuego. If I ever become rich, I'm going to move back to Guatemala and start my own brewery. I think it would be cool to name beers after volcanoes. Fuego would be an amber beer. Pacaya would be a smooth lager. San Pedro would be a wheat beer. There are thirty-three volcanoes scattered throughout the country's western highlands. I doubt that running out of volcanoes would be a problem. The only problem with Sky Bar is that the prices are elevated because of the terrific view. We can't afford to stay for too long.

We decide on an Irish bar called Reilly's. Of course, the majority owner is actually Danish. Reilly's is touristy, but it draws a lot of Guatemalan girls. That's the only reason my friends and I keep coming back—to chase the local talent. It's also packed on the weekends, and they play good music. Reasonably priced bar food is also served here. What more could a poor PCV ask for?

Initially, I hated Antigua. The place was too touristy and uneventful for me. I thought there was nothing to do here but drink and spend half my monthly stipend in two nights. I'm still right about the latter, but I love Antigua now. It took me a year to figure this out; I can always have fun here. I love Antigua because I know the place so well. I love Antigua because this is where I usually meet up with friends. Here we can forget that we are Peace Corps volunteers for a couple days. In Antigua, we are on vacation. And I have met all kinds of interesting people here. Except for Las Ramblas in Barcelona, I know of no finer place to people watch. The city has grown on me. I would like to own property here someday.

DECEMBER 19, 2007

Today I help Diego create a Yahoo! e-mail account. He decides on his password and username; diego.ramirez71 is now an active player on the information superhighway. Internet users, I advise you to proceed with caution. I set everything up for Diego. Then he practices logging on. We are at an Internet café, so I sit at another computer and send him a couple e-mails from my Gmail account. His face lights up when he sees the number "2" in his inbox. He replies with such enthusiasm. Diego is thirty-four years old. We spent around ninety minutes total. Afterward, I buy him lunch at Comedor Lupita. Diego orders fried chicken and I have *carne asada,* a roasted beef dish.

DECEMBER 24, 2007: STITCHED UP IN THE NEBAJ HOSPITAL

Work is over for the year. Chris and I go out drinking; we don't have anything else going on. Both of us have already read for several hours today. Nebaj does not offer much in terms of nightlife, but we are bored … and thirsty. We start the night off at El Descanso—the rooftop bar is open tonight. Chris and I are the only ones up there. We decide move on to the pool hall after a few Gallos. Chris and I walk home at around 2:30 a.m. We part ways at the gas station; we will hang out tomorrow for sure. It's Christmas. I am outside my house a few minutes later, and only then do I realize that I must have left my keys inside. Getting into the house is a two-step process. First, I must unlock the garage door, getting me inside. After that, I unlock the actual door to the house with a different key. No one else is home. Lynn has gone back to the United States for the holidays. I am sure that he left a spare key with one of the masons, but it's now 3:00 a.m. Everybody's cell phone is turned off at this hour.

I try to scale the wall on the side of the house. There are two problems with this. The first problem is that the wall is a little too tall for me. My shoes are too worn out to get any traction and scale it. The second and more serious problem is that the top of the wall is covered with broken glass. Years ago, a bunch of tools were stolen from Lynn's house, so he placed shards of glass around the entire perimeter to deter thieves. Since the glass has gone up, he's had no problems. I would soon learn why.

After thirty minutes with no success, I find a spot along the wall where the soil is elevated. I decide to try my luck there. Within minutes, my hand is on top of the wall. I have done it. I will scale this thing. I slide down yet again, but I feel confident that I will be on the other side within minutes. That's when I notice the blood, lots of it. I must have nicked my hand on a shard of glass. It's more than a nick; I am losing a lot of blood. I take off my long-sleeve Patagonia layer, using it to stanch the bleeding. Within a few minutes, the shirt is drenched with blood. I am starting to worry. I need to stop this bleeding, but I can't. I wonder if the hospital is open. If it isn't, I'll have to stay up until 5:30 a.m. and then catch a micro to Quiché. I know they have a decent hospital there.

I am going to try the Nebaj hospital anyway. Sweating profusely and bleeding a good bit, I decide to call Chris. I hope he's not asleep. I'd feel more comfortable walking with somebody.

"Yo."

"Hey Mullen."

"Yes sir, what's up?"

"I left my house keys inside. I've been trying to scale that cement wall on the side of the house for the last thirty minutes."

"How is that going?"

"Not well. That's why I'm calling. Will you meet me in front of your house in five minutes? I cut my wrist on one of those shards of glass. It's bleeding like crazy, and I think I need stitches. I'd just feel a little better walking to the hospital with someone else. Just in case something happens, you know."

"No worries, dude, swing by and we'll head up there."

I meet up with Chris three minutes later.

"How far of a walk is it?"

"I'm not exactly sure. It's outside of town. Maybe fifteen or twenty minutes from here."

"All right, thanks, Mullen."

"No problem, man. Let me have a look at that cut.… Oh, wow. Yeah, you definitely need stitches. I'd say at least eight. Those beers are not helping either. You're bleeding like crazy."

"Hey Mullen …"

"Yeah Taylor."

"Let's not tell anybody about this. This is some pretty good *chisme* that I don't want to get back to the Peace Corps office."

"Don't worry about that. My lips are sealed. You are right, though. This is one of those incidents that would get you some alcohol counseling sessions for sure."

The hospital looks deserted when we show up. Thankfully, it is open. A doctor from Chimaltenango is currently on duty. He quickly stitches me up. Surprisingly, I do not owe any money. As I reenter the waiting room, I show Chris my wrist. He tells me that those five stitches could have easily been ten. I tell him this is better than nothing. He and I are walking back to his house now. It's 5:00 a.m. I'll figure out how to get inside tomorrow.

DECEMBER 29, 2007: ANTIGUA

J. P., Eric, and I attend a party hosted by J. P.'s friend, Philip. Philip lives in a sumptuous gated community outside Antigua.

On paper, he exemplifies the Guatemalan elite: half-American, half-Guatemalan, owns five homes, runs three small business, Wharton MBA, et cetera. However, he's a very down-to-earth guy. So our plan is to enjoy this party, stay up until 5:00 a.m., and then catch our shuttle to Honduras.

After the party, our shuttle driver picks us up nearly two hours late. Then we discover that J. P. has lost our tickets. We arrive at the bus station with little time to spare, and we still haven't found our tickets. Latin American inefficiencies are helpful at times. A blatant disregard for the law is not always a bad thing. Breaking rules does not necessarily mean irreparable damage has been done. I approach the ticket counter and explain our situation. The man dryly replies that there are no exceptions. Travelers must have tickets in hand or they will not be allowed to board the bus. I think for a moment, frustrated and tired. I decide to try another way. J. P. and Eric are restively waiting behind me. We've got to get on this bus.

"Escuche señor."

"Si, dígame."

"Somos voluntarios del Cuerpo de Paz."

"Cuerpo de Paz."

"Pues sí, es una organización americana. Trabajamos aquí en su país—ayudando a los pobres. Nosotros llevamos casi dos años en Guatemala. Y no hemos ganado nada. Solamente nos gustaría disfrutar de la playa en Honduras por un par de días."

I throw a copy of my Peace Corps passport on the counter to corroborate my story. The guy is thinking.

"Vaya pues, ¿cuáles son sus apellidos?"

"Schroeder, Gibbons, y Dibbert- S-C-H-R-O-E-D-E-R, G-I-B-B-O-N-S, y D-I-B-B-E-R-T."

"Vaya, aquí están. Salen pronto."

"Muchísimas gracias señor, que pase un buen día."

"Igualmente."

"Listen, sir."

"Yep, tell me."

"We are Peace Corps volunteers."

"Peace Corps."

"Yes, it's an American organization. We work here in your country, helping the poor. We've lived in Guatemala for nearly two years. And we haven't earned any money. We would just like to enjoy the beach in Honduras for a couple of days."

"Alright, what are your last names?"

"Schroeder, Gibbons and Dibbert."

"Okay, here you go. Leave quickly."

"Thanks a lot sir. Have a good day."

"Same to you."

I quickly grab our tickets and walk outside before the guy has time to change his mind.

"Taylor, I don't know what you said to him, but thank you."

"Nice work, Dibbs."

"No worries, fellas, let's get on this bus."

I feel like James Bond. Nothing can stop us. Our Honduran vacation has begun. Priceless memories are inevitable. As the bus pulls out, I explain to Eric and J. P. that I merely told the guy that we were Peace Corps volunteers. I told him that we had lived here for nearly two years and hadn't earned a dime. I told him that we all live in indigenous towns. I told him that we just wanted to enjoy the beach for a few days. I told him the truth.

We arrive in La Ceiba that evening and are on the beach in Roatán the following day. The Bay Islands are internationally famous for inexpensive diving, but we weren't feeling that ambitious and decided that snorkeling was all we were up for. The beach was pristine, much better than anything Guatemala has to offer. Salva Vida, the local Honduran brew, blows Gallo out of the water. Copán, on the other hand, was a disappointment. We tried to go out there and had little success. The place is just too small, as if it were an Antigua for middle-school kids, though the ruins outside of town were pretty cool. Overall, although J. P., Eric, and I had a great time in Honduras, none of us are looking to return anytime soon. Frequent traveling breeds arrogance. The more you

155

see, the more difficult it is to be impressed when visiting a new place. Eric, J. P., and I had already seen a lot of Central America, so Honduras was unimpressive.

With frequent traveling also comes disdain for those Americans or Western Europeans who know little about the countries or regions that they are visiting. A couple nights ago in Roatán, I met a nice man from Ohio at a bar. He overheard that we were Peace Corps volunteers and offered to buy me a beer. I was delighted. He asked where we were "stationed." I said Guatemala. He quickly retorted that he had been to the Galápagos Islands. I was a bit confused; I did not see the relevance, but he quickly cleared things up for me.

"You see, Taylor, the Galápagos Islands are in Ecuador. They also speak Spanish there."

"Right. Well, Ecuador is a bit further south than Guatemala is, sir."

"Oh, well. All these countries are more or less the same. I guess the beer's a little different."

Then it hits me. This man actually believes that what he is saying is true. He has no idea that Guatemala is a highly diverse country with a rich cultural history, or that twenty-three indigenous languages are spoken there. Nor does he know that Honduras is quite different from Guatemala. There are almost no indigenous people in Honduras; the Spanish wiped them out. There are few indigenous people in El Salvador for the same reason. Costa Rica is a different story altogether. Ecotourism in Costa Rica is a model that all other Central American countries would like to follow. And Panama is arguably the most developed of all the Central American nations. I have excluded Mexico. And I haven't even gotten to South America yet. Of course there would be similarities among the various Latin American countries, but the differences are vast. Just like there are differences between the fifty states in the United States. International travel educates people when it compels them to continue to learn more about the world, when it forces them to realize that all countries are unique and special in their own right. But it can also be a waste of time and money.

I thank the man for the beer and excuse myself. I am on vacation; I am not up for teaching that night.

Fifteen: Xepiun, Baztaja, Xebe, and Vicalamá

January 9, 2008: Xepiun

Diego, Peter, and I are doing a water survey in Xepiun today. This is Peter's first legitimate field experience in Guatemala, so I let him do most of the work. He measures the change in altitude with the Abney level, he uses the compass to find our orientation, he asks for the distance from point to point, and he records all of this information. The night before, I told Peter not to worry about lunch. I told him that we are always given lunch. We are doing the community a huge favor. They desperately need a water system.

Of course, today we are not given lunch. This blows my mind. This is the first time it's happened to me since I moved to Nebaj. Providing lunch to development workers has almost been codified into law in the Ixil Triangle. We do the water surveys for free. Diego does receive a modest monthly salary, but the Westerners are never paid. The villagers know that. I am even more shocked because one of the Agua Para la Salud masons, Nicolas Bernal, was born and raised in Xepiun. He still lives here. I'm really, really unhappy. And as my dear friends and sweet mother know, I turn into a mean and terse person when I don't get my Happy Meal at lunch. I don't speak much until we start walking to the car at the end of the day. A little after four o'clock, Peter and I stop by Don's for a meal. After an enormous beef burrito, I am my normal happy self again.

JANUARY 11, 2008

Lynn and I are in Batzaja this morning. We will be starting a water-system project there this spring. Math remains a relatively new phenomenon in rural Guatemala. In most of the *tiendas* in the western highlands, people use pocket calculators or multiplication tables to solve even the most basic math problems. Lynn and I spend two hours explaining the importance of using right angles when measuring. A lack of basic math has been creating all kinds of problems up here. People are getting cheated on business transactions when they are buying land. People are getting incorrect change when they purchase items at the market or in a store. I could go on. As ESPN's Nick Bakay once said, "The numbers never lie."

JANUARY 15, 2008

I am at Don's for dinner; I will be enjoying a grilled-cheese and fries shortly. I quickly give him my order and head for the bathroom to wash my hands. I walk in on two young Ixils—a guy is hitting a girl in Don's bathroom. I should have smacked the guy between the eyes, but instead I do nothing. I just glare. I don't need a fight at a popular restaurant and hostel in my hometown. I don't want to get in trouble. Rumors fly in the Peace Corps. I share secrets with few people and confide only in close friends. If word got out that I assaulted a guy in my town, I'd be on a plane back to the United States by mid-February. Or maybe I am just a coward. I feel guilty for not doing anything; I don't want to risk it. I've been down here for nearly two years. I don't want to get booted out now.

I've got other things on my mind as I walk back to my house with a belly full of food. On a more confusing note, I think I have a crush on Anna Karenina. It would be great if there were a beautiful, intelligent Ixil woman named Anna Karenina, but I'm referring to the literary character. She's so wonderful. And I'm *so* lonely. How I long for the touch of a woman. But not just any woman, someone cultured, sophisticated, worldly. I would strongly prefer that she be Southern, but I'm too desperate to be that picky at the moment. Maybe I'm destined for a life of pensive solitude. After all, love is not for everyone; some must be left outside its gates. I suspect that I am one of them, condemned to a loveless life. Although, I am still relatively young, so I may have a chance. All I can do is hope. I'm not sure what part of my brain is producing this circuitous internal monologue. I just know that I need sleep. When I get home, I brush my teeth and crash immediately.

JANUARY 27, 2008

All week, Peter and I have been in Santa María Chiquimula in the department of Totonicapán near Xela. I immediately notice how dry it is here. I had forgotten that Ixil country is the anomaly. It's dry pretty much everywhere this time of year.

PCV Kody Gerkin lives here. Kody is a friend of mine from training. He called Lynn a couple of weeks ago. Kody needs someone to do a water survey in one of the villages near his site—Xebe. So Lynn asked Peter and me to take care of it. We are happy to do it. Kody appreciates the favor and cooks dinner for us every night this week. It's Friday, and Peter and I have finished the survey. We have had great weather all week. Peter and I are both looking a little sunburned. And we have done Kody a huge favor; in the eyes of these villagers, he looks like a stud. The three of us decide to celebrate in Xela that night. We call and reserve a room at Casa Argentina before we leave Kody's house.

FEBRUARY 7, 2008

Peter, Diego, and I are sleeping at the only "hotel" in Vicalamá tonight. A "hotel" in isolated Vicalamá looks a lot like a dilapidated toolshed in the United States, although I assume that the dirt floor in our room is cleaner than most in the area. The entire room smells like corn tortillas and refried beans; we are right next to the kitchen. The three beds are small but sufficient. The cost is five quetzales per person per night. I wake up because I smell smoke. I see flames near my head. These flames are coming through the thin wooden boards separating our room from the kitchen. I am sure that Peter and Diego are able to hear lots of frenetic chattering in Ixil. I have not yet taken my earplugs out. By the time I do, the flames have subsided. Smoke permeates our bedroom. We step outside for some fresh air. Apparently, an electrical wire started the fire. Most houses in Vicalamá do not have electricity, making the fire especially surprising. Peter, Diego, and I are too tired to think about it. The smoke clears quickly. We are back in bed fifteen minutes later.

EARLY MARCH, 2008

There are some Appropriate Technology (AT) committee meetings in Xela. Basilio Estrada runs the AT program. Within Peace Corps, he holds the title of Associate Peace Corps Director (APCD). Each APCD is in charge of a specific program, sometimes two. Basilio is involved in Peace Corps training and site selection for new volunteers. He also collaborates with various NGOs and health groups in the country, effectively putting a PCV with a counterpart agency. Out of concern for the direction and viability of the Appropriate Technology program in Guatemala, Basilio has organized a small committee of PCVs to help him modify our program. A new AT group is sent to Guatemala every year. Basilio picks two or three people from each group to assist him throughout their service. I accepted Basilio's offer because I do think my program could be improved. I also like to debate and discuss problems with other people. Lastly, all AT committee meetings are held in one of two Peace Corps hubs: COFA in Xela or in Santa Lucía, Sacatepéquez. So PCVs will sleep in Xela or Antigua and have all their expenses paid. AT committee members Anthony and Gwen, both from the training group behind mine, become close friends. Our meetings go well. Everyone comes ready to work, and we accomplish a lot in two days.

MID-MARCH, 2008

I'm in Antigua for some Peace Corps meetings. One of those meetings is with my APCD, Basilio Estrada. I had scheduled this one about a month ago. I want him to explain what I would be doing as a PCV leader if I choose to stay in country for an additional six to twelve months. The meeting is not that helpful; Basilio answers some of my questions evasively. I will probably finish with Peace Corps in July. I leave Santa Lucía Milpas Altas at 5:00 p.m. I am exhausted. I patiently wait for a ride back to Antigua. This time, I will not be traveling in a camioneta. Antigua-Guatemala City camionetas have not been running for the past thirty-six hours. This means that no camionetas will be passing by Santa Lucía either. The reason: a driver and an *ayudante* were shot and killed yesterday morning. Clearly, this was gang-related. Other people will still be giving rides. I jump into the back of a pickup at 5:30 p.m. By 6:00 p.m. I am back at the Burkhardt. I am ready for a hot shower and some cable television. Tonight I am going to eat chicken curry at Travel Menu, my favorite restaurant in Antigua. This is exhilarating for someone who has been living in Nebaj since August of 2006.

When some people think of Guatemala, they think of peasants rioting in the streets, massacres in urban areas, drug abuse, gang activity, and a weak education system. Many people may not give the country even that much thought. They may know that Spanish is spoken there, but they would probably have no idea that twenty-three indigenous languages are also spoken. They may have heard of Guatemala's tragic thirty-six-year civil war, but they would not know that Guatemala is a place of unsurpassable beauty and a nation replete with natural resources. They may wonder why Guatemala rarely receives any attention from the international media. Many people would never bother visiting the place. "Why not just go to Mexico?"

Statistically speaking, Guatemala is a violent country. Like many other countries, the country has a history of violence. However, I have felt safe at all times in Guatemala, with my encounter with thieves in Guatemala City being the one exception. In Nebaj, I have felt extremely safe at all times.

Nevertheless, gangs are a problem here. Whenever I buy a *Presna Libre*—the country's most widely circulated newspaper—there are at least a couple of articles devoted to gang-related violence in the capital. I realize that a disproportionate amount of the violence takes place in Guatemala City. The US State Department, on its website, advises travelers to avoid several Zonas in the capital. Gang-related violence is the principal reason for this. Peace Corps volunteers are not even allowed to spend the night out in Guatemala City, unless they sleep in one of about five or six hotels that Peace Corps Guatemala considers acceptable. Going by the Guatemalan government's Human Rights Ombudsman's Office, homicides in Guatemala rose by 40 percent from 2001 to 2004. During that time, Guatemala's homicide rate was thirty-five per 100,000 inhabitants. If this sounds like a relatively low number, it certainly is not. The homicide rate in the United States during the same period was less than six per 100,000 inhabitants. If violence in Guatemala were curbed dramatically over the course of the next decade, it would still be deemed a violent or relatively unsafe place by world standards. And nobody expects those numbers to improve anytime soon anyway.

The two biggest gangs in the country are Mara Salvatrucha, also known as MS-13, and 18th Street, or just 18. Guatemala is a prime location for gang recruitment. The country has an extremely young population. Unemployment and underemployment are huge problems here. The education system does not function smoothly. In Guatemala, most of the gang members are poor and probably ladino. But that doesn't mean there's not gang activity outside the major urban areas. Cotzal, the second biggest city in the Ixil Triangle, is known for gang violence. Nebaj is quite calm. I frequently see gang-related graffiti on the town's outskirts, though. However, I have had no firsthand knowledge of gang-related activity in Guatemala.

MID-MARCH, 2008: MY PARENTS VISIT

My parents will spend the next two nights with me in Nebaj. I have been looking forward to this. Today we hike up to a spring box in Batzaja. I designed their water system and Agua Para la Salud recently helped them build it. It is both interesting and funny to witness my parents' observations about Cocop, a small model village we pass through on our way to the spring site. They quickly note that the women carry everything on their heads, and that they make it look so easy. They comment on the high volume at which villagers listen to the radio. I tell them that the portable radios are rechargeable. You just have to twist a lever; I don't know if there's electricity out here. We also see men, women, and children carrying firewood up the mountain. They have tied the wood in a bundle and then connected that bundle to a strap attached to their foreheads. The bundles of wood now hang behind them, near their lower backs. I tell my parents that during water projects, I have even seen men haul bags of cement using this method. I once tried it with a few pieces of wood; the pain was unbearable. It creates incredible pressure on one's neck. My parents are amazed at what they see.

These are aspects of my life that I no longer notice. I still hear the radio programs in Ixil and the loud music, but it no longer bothers me. I still hear all the honking of horns and the bleating of animals, but don't care. I still hear the "singing" in Evangelical churches, but I no longer shake my head in disdain as I walk through the streets of Nebaj. Most people do not know that churches in rural Guatemala are among the world's noisiest. The *chuchos* barking in the street no longer annoy me. When I see them, I conspicuously pretend that I'm bending over to pick up a rock. Those pitiful street dogs either pipe down or run away immediately. I have grown accustomed to so much. I have adjusted to my environment accordingly.

The following evening, we have dinner at the Maya Ixil, a nice restaurant—by Nebaj standards—located just north of the main square. Four of the five masons have come. Of course, I am not including Dionysio, since I did not invite him. Josh and Chris are also attending. Peter is out of town, so unfortunately my parents won't get to meet him. The dinner is interesting. Previously, I had told my parents that all of the masons are married. During dinner, my dad wants me to ask them about a typical Ixil wedding. I have to briefly explain that most marriages in the Ixil Triangle are common-law marriages. People do not necessarily have an official ceremony because they can't afford it. Explaining none of the previous conversations to the masons, I change the subject and mention that my parents got a look at the Batzaja water system yesterday. This goes over quite well; these men take great pride in their work. Antonio even presents my mother with a gorgeous multicolored shawl that his wife has made. This is a traditional, yet very nice gesture on his part. My mom feels very honored.

My parents know no Spanish outside of the words *hola* and *gracias*. Diego can speak some English, though he is usually reluctant to use it in public. The masons have worked with Westerners before, though they said that never before had they met both parents of a volunteer. I was proud of my parents for coming all the way out here. Ixil country is place of unsurpassable natural beauty, a fascinating history, and warm, friendly people. Sadly, if all Americans were given a world map, I doubt many could find Guatemala quickly. Locating Nebaj, an indigenous town in the western highlands, would be exponentially more difficult. The past two days, my parents have witnessed things that most Americans will never even read about, much less experience firsthand.

We have just arrived in Guatemala City. My father hired a private driver to take us, a brilliant idea. I can't imagine my mom ever using the public transportation in this country. I am staying at the Westin Camino Real in Guatemala City with Mom and Dad tonight. The hotel is located in Zona 10, a very nice neighborhood in the capital. I am excited to see them, but right now I can't stop thinking about my Westin heavenly bed and the terrific shower. I don't ever want to leave my hotel room.

We fly to Tikal early the next morning. Located in the northern part of Guatemala in El Petén, Tikal is one of the biggest Mayan archaeological sites. Tikal is what most people think of when they think of Guatemala—big pyramids in the jungle. At the peak of Mayan civilization, Tikal was one of the most important cities. At the ruins, the most impressive structures are the six-step pyramids. At the peak of each pyramid lies a summit. Some of the pyramids are more than two hundred feet high. The pictures of them look so impressive, I can't wait to climb a couple of them.

MARCH 21, 2008

I am at Tikal with my parents and our guide, Mario. My shirt is drenched with sweat, and we have only been walking around for an hour. There isn't a cloud in sight; the heat will continue unabated. We are only spending one night at the Jungle Lodge outside of the national park. They use generators at the hotel, but still only have about nine hours of electricity per day. My mom is not amused. She's ready for the Porta Hotel in Antigua, and we haven't even been here for ten hours.

After tonight, we will fly back to Guatemala City. They will fly home in a couple of days. I will enjoy Antigua for one more night and then head back to Nebaj early the following morning. I am glad my parents have caught a glimpse of my Guatemalan life. E-mails and phone conversations are great, yet insufficient. They needed to actually visit the country in order to fully understand. I wonder how they'll feel when they get home.

EARLY APRIL, 2008

Diego and I are checking our schematic design for a water system in La Libertad. We had finished our water survey in La Libertad last week, and I did the schematic design yesterday. But now several additional people want to be involved in the water project.

Since they are willing to work, each additional household will get a spigot right to their back porch. Diego and I need to locate these houses so that our schematic design includes all beneficiaries. Otherwise, our material list will not be accurate. We work hard all morning and finish our work. Then we have lunch with a family and drive back to Nebaj that afternoon. For lunch, we were each given one hard-boiled egg and a stack of tortillas. I must add that my hard-boiled egg was cooked perfectly.

APRIL 9, 2008: SOLOLÁ

About fifteen members of Wisconsin Water for the World, an NGO, have arrived. I cannot believe we are sleeping at the hotel Don Beto at Los Encuentros. Los Encuentros is the most important highway junction in Guatemala. Situated along the Inter-American Highway, it's a disgusting place. The area is teeming with dirty comedores and *tiendas*. There is also an abundance of street vendors here, peddling anything from french fries to fried plantains, fresh fruit, soft drinks, tamales, or newspapers. There's also a small army base here. Because of all the traffic, air becomes opaque here. If I don't pay attention, I'm likely to get a mouthful of exhaust smoke while waiting to make my connection. This is not a pleasant place to spend the night, but Lynn has decided that it makes sense logistically.

We will be working in El Adelanto, a nearby village. The project involves building a water system and also health education. The project will last for three months, but the Wisconsin Water for the World people will be in country for only about two weeks. Most of them still work full-time; obviously, nobody can take three months off to do development work down here. Three other PCVs and I will be working on the project. We are needed primarily for our language skills. Lynn has meticulously planned all aspects of the project. Each PCV will work with a group of Wisconsin Water for the World volunteers.

El Adelanto has been all right so far. I could not imagine working here without Felipe, Stephanie, and Tony.

I am attending a "TRANS" Party in Santa Cruz la Laguna on the lake this weekend. I am not sure if the word "TRANS" stands for transvestite or transsexual. Either way, I will be wearing a dress and maybe even a wig. These parties are held every Saturday at the Iguana Perdida, the only hostel worth staying at in an otherwise boring town. Basically, everyone dresses up, eats an excellent buffet dinner, and has an enjoyable evening.

I haven't worn a dress since I was "asked" to wear one by some older fraternity brothers in the fall of 2001. I was a pledge at the time. I didn't mind the dress, but wearing high heels nearly killed me. I took them off after a couple of hours, however it still took me a week to recover from the experience.

At the Iguana Perdida, they have a wide selection of dresses to choose from. Since I am classy, I go with something simple, a little black dress. Anthony, my roommate for the night, chooses a light-blue beauty. It looks like something my grandmother would have worn in the 1970s. Apparently, Anthony feels uncomfortable about his small breasts, because he stuffs his chest with toilet paper shortly after we change. At least he doesn't shave his chest. The party is great. About fifteen PCVs are in attendance, most of whom live near Lake Atitlán. The following morning, Stephanie, Felipe, Anthony, and I eat a delicious breakfast and catch a *lancha* back to Panajachel. From there, we take a camioneta back to Los Encuentros. We still have another week of work with Wisconsin Water for the World in El Adelanto.

APRIL 17, 2008: PANAJACHEL

Stephanie, Anthony, and I go out in Panajachel. Panajachel has been nicknamed Gringolandia. The place is so touristy, and there's really just one major street to walk down. I've never been a big fan. Nevertheless , it's always nice to go out with Stephanie Kollar and Anthony Hicks, two people whose company I greatly enjoy. Both of them are also in the Appropriate Technology program; they arrived in country a year after I did. Stephanie is from Chicago, and Tony grew up in South Carolina. There are few Southerners down here, so it's especially nice to have Tony around. He speaks both college and professional football fluently. He's also proficient in baseball. Aside from sports, we normally have a lot to talk about anyway.

I consider Panajachel the second most overrated city in Guatemala, behind Chichicastenango, the place known for having the most impressive market in the country. I am not a big shopper, so big markets do not interest me. Some will say that Lake Atitlán is beautiful and that is why they are visiting "Pana." Of course the lake is beautiful. No one is debating that. In fact, Aldous Huxley once described it as "the most beautiful lake in the world." I don't know if he had eaten any acid the day he said that, but I will assume he was thinking clearly enough.

The point is this: For a nice, relaxing time on Lake Atitlán, one should avoid Panajachel unless he or she is a highly inexperienced traveler. And besides, Pana isn't directly on the water. The ugly dock obstructs the view of the lake unless one is sitting at the Sunset Café at the end of Calle Santander. I should add that the Sunset Café is an excellent place to have a few drinks for those people content with staying in Pana.

For dinner that night, we buy fried chicken and fries from a street vendor for 10Q a plate. This is fine, since we were all looking for a cheap, greasy option that evening. Later we watch some live music at PanaRock. The band covers mostly Maná songs, which we all enjoy. The three of us stroll back to Casa Linda, our quaint hotel just off of Calle Santander, Pana's main drag. Anthony is exhausted and goes straight to bed. Stephanie and I stay up for a couple more hours. We talk about all kinds of stuff—politics, Guatemalan history, the Peace Corps bureaucracy, and the top spots for happy hour in Antigua, among other things. Stephanie is bright and engaging and fun to talk to. Good conversation is precious. Neither of us wants our chat to end. Unfortunately, we need sleep. The next morning, the three of us grab breakfast together and then head back to our respective sites.

APRIL 19, 2008: SATURDAY

And I live yet another typical Saturday in Nebaj. My walk to the waterfall is more enjoyable when I have been out of town for an extended period to time. I meander down the old road to Chajul for about a half an hour and then usually turn back shortly thereafter. The walk always helps me to gather my thoughts and think clearly.

I try to find a pair of shorts for my upcoming trip to El Salvador, but all efforts prove fruitless. Strangely, I stumble upon a nice Wordsworth anthology at one of the PACA stores. Is all great literature in Nebaj buried deep in musty bags of secondhand clothing? I buy the book for only five quetzales. Maybe my shopping adventure *was* a success.

APRIL 29, 2008: EL ZONTE, EL SALVADOR

I have been enjoying *Green Hills of Africa*. Hemingway was terrified of snakes. I am in good company. He was also an outstanding conversationalist. I love hearing him "speak" about art. He says that art is the only lasting endeavor. It's true—great works of art do live on. The cool kids in high school will be listening to Led Zeppelin forever. Millions of people flock to the Sistine Chapel each year without end. The same must be said for the works of Pablo Picasso; I will never tire of staring at his paintings. And Humphrey Bogart's films will be revered ceaselessly. The same can be said for the works of Dostoyevsky or Tolstoy or Fitzgerald or Borges or Conrad or Hemingway himself. And again I must mention Pablo Neruda's poetry. Never before have I been so moved by so few words. There is no scarcity of beauty and artistic excellence in this world. It is merely a matter of looking in the right places.

This weekend I am in El Salvador (La Libertad) with some friends: Walker, James, and Eric. We are staying at a place called Horizonte in El Zonte, on the Pacific coast. We went out in one of the neighboring towns, Tunco, last night. It was just a big sausage party. La Libertad is a laid-back place with weak nightlife and underwhelming, rocky beaches. This is a place to surf and get stoned, which is not our style. The lack of girls notwithstanding, we had a good time and got some sun. Admittedly, the trip probably would have been cooler if we were surfers.

MAY 6, 2008: NEBAJ

I eat dinner with Chris at my place, and we speak about our respective English classes. My lukewarm success can hardly be compared to his utter brilliance with regard to this matter. Admittedly, Chris has been teaching in Nebaj for a year and a half. I have only been teaching since November. Some of his students can converse on an advanced level. My students can construct only the most basic sentences. And my classes are much smaller than his. I only teach a few young people who work at El Descanso, including Rosa.

Unfortunately, Rosa's interest has quickly evaporated. She's breaking my heart. I realize that there can be only one logical explanation: the girl was forced, either implicitly or explicitly, to stop attending. I do not think that individual classes with her were a good idea.

On one occasion, she even brought her little brother! Perhaps she will do anything to avoid a scandalous moment with a handsome gringo. I know that her parents are really strict. I mean, the girl's curfew is 8:00 p.m. And she is twenty! I am quite sure she is still single. Maybe some jealous boys have influenced her decision. A few of the guys have been noticeably less friendly since I started giving classes, in spite of the fact that they have also attended more than a few of my English classes. Who knows? I just wanted to help the Nebajeños. I have worked almost exclusively in the villages during my two years. Our NGO maintains an office in Nebaj, but we don't actually build water systems or rainwater-catchment tanks in Nebaj. Sure, Nebaj is behind. There are a lot of poor people, but at least everybody in Nebaj has access to potable water. The villages outside of Nebaj are much worse off.

MAY 13, 2008

As I watch the movie *Love in the Time of Cholera*, I am reminded that a book is always better, more complete than the film version. This is especially true in terms of character development. The suspense derived from great writing can seldom be developed as well in movies. Plus, García Márquez's amazing command of the language—the elegant and special prose that only the most talented writers can create—cannot be completely transformed into a movie.

MAY 19, 2008

Unfortunately, I have had a huge falling out with Agua Para la Salud employee Dionysio Gaspar. Dionysio works primarily as an accountant. He coordinates material purchases for our projects in the villages. We buy materials like PVC pipes, cement, and rebar from a supplier in Guatemala City or Xela.

Dionysio happens to be the only Evangelical we have working at our NGO. He is deeply religious. He does not drink. He does not smoke. He claims he has the moral high ground on every issue because of his abstemious ways. Yet paradoxically, he has trouble telling the truth. This has been a difficult situation for me, because the guy has worked with Lynn for about ten years. In some ways, Dionysio is an asset at our NGO. He is a bit of an ass and can be a tough negotiator when he has to. The skills are helpful when haggling over material costs or discussing a work contract with villagers. However, the man routinely alters my material lists after I have already turned them in. I was at the office rewriting material lists until 7:00 p.m. because of him. He also happens to be the only accountant I have ever met who simply cannot count. Before I turned in a disc of project information to him, I should have locked my spreadsheets up so that he couldn't alter them. I will be working in Nebaj through July, though not with him.

"Hey Lynn, it's Taylor."

"Hello, Taylor. Is this about Dionysio?"

"Did he already call you?"

"Well, I had called him about an unrelated issue in Xemamatze, and he mentioned that you and he had a little discussion."

"I am shocked that he would refer to it as a 'discussion.' It doesn't really matter though, Lynn. I have committed to work at this NGO until the end of July, which I am happy to do. But I will not work with Dionysio another day. I would just like to turn in all my budgetary proposals and material lists directly to you. Dionysio is a liar."

"Well, look, Taylor. I know that you are frustrated. But I've been working with Dionysio a long time. I know that he can be stubborn, but the man usually finds a way to get things done. Sometimes it's a good thing when the guy crunching the numbers is a bit stubborn."

"Lynn, with all due respect, this has nothing to do with Dionysio being stubborn. I don't want to work with him anymore because he is a liar. Plain and simple. He has been changing my material lists for too long, and then he lies to me about it. This isn't even deceitful lying, Lynn. It's blatant, and I've let this go on for too long. Then Dionysio starts telling me about how he's an Evangelical, and that he's a good person. And that I should trust him. Just because he thinks he lives an ascetic life doesn't mean he can just lie. It's really absurd."

"I understand how you feel Taylor. Why don't we talk about this in greater detail when I get back to Nebaj this week? I have to go look at a couple of schools in Sololá over the next couple of days, so I won't be back until Sunday afternoon."

"That sounds good, Lynn."

"Okay, Taylor, you take care."

"Yep, you too."

Lynn Roberts is unflappable. He has been working in Guatemala for so long. The man has seen everything. I've rarely seen him lose his temper, perhaps less than five times these past two years. I am glad I spoke with him today. I needed to get it off my chest. Lynn is such a good man. He'll be my toughest hug come late July.

MAY 26, 2008

Erik Joseph, a friend of mine from upstate New York, is visiting this weekend. Unfortunately, Erik did his undergraduate work at the University of Florida. However, I am convinced that he is the coolest guy ever to come out of that school. In the spring of 2005, we participated in the same study-abroad program in Valencia, Spain, and have kept in touch since then.

Erik and I hit all the major spots in Antigua, at least as far as nightlife goes. We have a great time. Erik never even got sick. He did make out with a seventeen-year-old girl named Andrea at Studio 54, near the famous arch just off the *parque*. She was gorgeous, too. Even funnier, Andrea was a senior in high school. She and a few friends were on a mother-daughter trip that evening. All the girls live in Guatemala City. Erik figured this out because they abruptly left right at midnight. Erik decided to walk them outside, and he saw a white Suburban outside. A couple of the moms had decided to pick their kids up in front of the bar. I couldn't believe it when he told me.

We stopped by an after-party on Saturday as well. Antigua after-parties are hit or miss. Some are great, and others are terribly boring. Last night, we should have won the Pub Quiz at Reilly's; we lost by one point. We had the question on the rise of oil prices right, but alas, we were not believed. It was even more frustrating because we lost to a group of arrogant Antigua expatriates. These are people who think they are special because they have won the pub quiz several times. The problem with this line of thinking is that they are usually the only ones attending that Pub Quiz several dozen times over the course of the year. Ergo, they are not as fancy as they think they are.

Erik was furious. He works at one of the major international banks in New York City. For the past three years, he has followed the financial markets and commodity prices on a daily basis. Both of us were certain that oil prices had risen approximately 50 percent over the past year. The other group thought that number was closer to 25 percent, and the little Cuban guy announcing the questions sided with them. He candidly told us that he didn't know, but that these questions had been pulled from the Internet by a close friend of his about a month or two ago, admitting that they weren't current. So we had the right answer, but we lost anyway.

Erik and I are recovering this afternoon, but it's only Sunday. He doesn't fly out until Monday morning, so I decide to spend an additional night in Antigua with him. At Café No Se, we both nurse hangovers as we half-heartedly eat our chicken quesadillas. I order my second Bloody Mary—they're excellent here—and start to worry about Erik. He's looking a little pale; it may just be the lack of sleep.

"Hey, what do you think of your Guatemalan experience? You're in town for the weekend from New York. You spend ten hours a day in a cubicle. You spend an hour and a half commuting to work every day. I am curious to know."

"Honestly, it's been awesome. Antigua is a really fun place. I would've liked to have seen more of the country, but I didn't want to be away from work for too long. And this has been really cheap."

"Yeah, compared to Manhattan, I have no doubt."

Erik is picked up at the Burkhardt at five o'clock the following morning. He has a 6:30 a.m. flight. He was my first visitor, besides my parents. It was great to see a friendly face. Only now do I realize how well I have gotten to know some of my fellow PCVs. I have met some amazing people, and I have made some lifelong friendships down here.

Sixteen: Fiesta of Sunset

Close of Service Conference in Antigua

Our entire training group will be in Antigua these next few days for our Close of Service conference. This is the last official meeting for our Peace Corps training group. Peace Corps administrators will discuss reports we need to file and medical examinations we need to schedule. We will be given information about our readjustment allowance. Each PCV will receive about $6,000 for successfully completing their service; PCVs accrue around $225 for every month of service in country. This money gives us time to get settled when we go back to the United States. Other people will use the money to travel throughout Latin America. Either way, it's a small yet greatly appreciated sum to fall back on for a little while. We will also listen to a presentation about a couple of low-cost health-insurance plans available for returned Peace Corps volunteers. Lastly, all of us will fill out surveys and give suggestions about Peace Corps Guatemala. The meetings are extremely boring, yet most PCVs look forward to their COS conference. First of all, this means that the end is near. For 99 percent of PCVs, twenty-seven months in Guatemala is more than enough. And secondly, our entire training group will be together for the last time. It's a time to socialize and reflect upon our two years of service.

Having been asked to speak at the conference, I said the following this morning at the Hotel Soleil in Antigua:

"I should start by saying that I would have planned my speech a little differently if I had known that only our training group and Country Director Jim Adriance would be attending. We should all be delighted to spend a couple nights at the elegant Hotel Soleil, though; I noticed that UNICEF is using the conference room next to ours today. If we have learned nothing else during our two years down here, we all know that when it comes to administrative costs, the UN spares no expense. This place must be one of the nicest in town.

"I wish Lynn Roberts were present, since he helped me so much over the course of my two years here. But that unflappable Guatemalan MacGyver was not invited. I have no doubt that Lynn Roberts will be my toughest hug when I leave Guatemala in July. Lynn is the most resourceful man in the world. If he were here now, he could probably make the chairs more comfortable or make the lighting better. At the very least, he would be wearing a festive vest and add some color to the crowd. For me, Lynn has been more like a father figure than a boss or a colleague, and he is such a great person, so hardworking and tireless. It has been a privilege and a pleasure; I would not have had nearly as good of an experience if he hadn't been in Nebaj.

"So, Country Director Jim Adriance called me last Friday and asked if I would say a couple things at the start of the conference. I said I would love to. He told me it is not a big deal, but that he would like for me to set the tone for the rest of the meetings. He then clarified that by saying that I should only feel pressure to set the tone, which sounds strangely like a pep talk. So to me it seems like the tone we will be going for during the next couple of days would be happiness and excitement. *Happiness*, pure joy really, since we will be leaving soon. And I know most of the people in this room are ready to move on. And *excitement*, since a lot of y'all are going to be doing some cool stuff upon finishing your service, and also because we get to stay at this sweet hotel and can hopefully go for free massages later.

"Before I say anything too weird, I should add that it is funny that I am up here speaking, since I am not very politically correct. I am not very diplomatic at all really, which leads me to the idea that I don't have anything to say that will be good enough for this crowd. For two years, y'all have lived voluntarily in some remote parts of Guatemala. Nothing I say will fully encapsulate this experience, which is fine. Events in your life might not always translate perfectly into words. This has been interesting. Frankly, the worst days of my life have been in this country, but there is no need to dwell on that. Clearly, the good days vastly exceeded the bad ones. This is a special group; I wonder how many times in the history of Peace Corps Guatemala a group had more extensions than early terminations. I would guess it had never happened until now.

"I mainly want to emphasize the following: the Peace Corps experience is an amazingly unique experience. I can safely say that I interpret the world very differently because I was a PCV in Guatemala. Guatemala is a mark on my life and my heart that will not come out. It's a permanent tattoo.

"I read an article in the Peace Corps *WorldView* magazine. Hooray for Peace Corps—we now have more PCVs than we have had in over thirty years, a number like 8,142. In 1966, there were 15,000 PCVs, the highest number ever. Those people doing public relations at the State Department have got to be so desperate. Less than 8,000 people, in a country of 300 million, is a tiny number. Since its inception in 1961, less than 200,000 people have served in the Peace Corps. Many know the name, yet few really *know* what the job entails.

"The life of a Peace Corps volunteer is an incomparable experience. Y'all should not let anyone tell you otherwise. It is funny to think that Peace Corps volunteers travel to some of the world's sketchiest places to live, but the journey is really more of an introspective one. I can personally say that I have found out a lot about myself these last two years. And really, coming down here was the single best decision I have ever made. I realize that I am only twenty-five, hoping to have some better decisions, but for now that is true. I'm telling y'all this, and I know all the secrets, I know one-third of everybody's time was spent reading books and drinking coffee. Yet still, 99.9 percent of Americans are not even up for that if it's gonna be in a place called San José Ojetenam or Chiquimula or Vásquez or Tecpán or Tejar."

FRIENDSHIPS

"I wish I could stand up here and tell you that I've got dozens of great Guatemalan friends. I wish I could say that I met my future wife down here. And that she was Guatemalan and hot. But I can't say that because I don't have any game, so I never could find my Guatemalan wife. I do have a few Guatemalan friends, and I will try to keep in touch with them, but the best friends I have are all in this room. We have seen and done stuff together that most people can only read about in magazines or see on the Discovery Channel for a fleeting moment. We forget how rare these experiences are since we are constantly sharing our experiences with each other. We have tricked ourselves into thinking we have ordinary or regular lives. Some of the more delusional individuals in this room may even describe themselves as normal. That assertion could not be more untrue.

"It is so important to have people to relate to and share the experience with. If someone sends me a text from the States, asking how my day was, how am I going to explain what it is like being hungover on a camioneta for eight hours on a Sunday, the last three of which are even more miserable because a baby has vomited on your shoulder?"

BE PROUD

"We should be proud of the work we did down here. I know that nobody managed to save the world, but at least we tried. I want to read a quote from my favorite book, *As a Man Thinketh*. The author, James Allen, talks about how human beings typically misinterpret the success of others. We may look at a famous actor or writer or wealthy banker and tell ourselves that those people are just lucky or smart or rich. Allen says: 'They do not see the trials and failures and struggles which these men and women have voluntarily encountered in order to gain their experience; have no knowledge of the sacrifices they have made, of the undaunted efforts they have put forth, of the faith they have exercised, that they might overcome the apparently insurmountable, and realize the Vision of their heart.'

"Basically, Allen is saying that people only perceive people's accomplishments and never look behind those successful people to see *how* and *why* they were successful. Fortuitous events occur far less often than we think. Nobody in this room was here by accident. To a certain extent, we all got exactly what we wanted. Coming down here for two years, y'all proved to yourselves that you can do whatever you want. When the people in this room go on to accomplish even more, that will not be coincidental. At the very least, everyone should feel they've been given a lifetime of self-confidence. And aren't we all extraordinarily appreciative of everything we have in the States? Just to have that peace of mind at any stage in life is invaluable. And so now we're here for two days to get a little closure on two unbelievable years, which is impossible. I know that I will need at least several months before I feel normal again. In fact, I may never feel normal again.

"And maybe I am harboring a few negative thoughts about Guatemala or about the Peace Corps, but really I think all of those negative things are not specific to Guatemala or to the Peace Corps. They're just problems that occur when you work in international development. International development work is not easy. And it is not pretty. That's kind of the point.

"Please pay attention to what you say to people in the States when y'all get back. Y'all will run into three kinds of people wanting to ask you about Peace Corps. There will be those who don't care, those that do care, and those who care because they are also thinking about making the leap. I would never discourage anyone from joining the Peace Corps. The people in this room have achieved so much. Running Internet cafés, working in various cooperatives, supporting women's groups, building stoves and latrines, marketing local products, teaching health and hygiene or English, and showing Guatemala's poor that that they are not alone, that Americans are willing and able to help.

"I know that later on, when we think about what we did down here, we will all have really fond memories of this place. We will have no doubt that this was the adventure of a lifetime. And we will know that this country, these people, and this job have forever changed our lives in a very positive way. Thanks for listening."

Since last Tuesday, I have been partying nonstop. Over the past four nights, I have slept about fourteen hours. I am thrilled about turning in early tonight. My Close of Service speech went well. I am certainly a better public speaker than I was two years ago.

I will never be able to get this life back after July. In some ways, I am not sure that I want to.

JUNE 2, 2008

Lynn has asked me to participate in one final field-based training. Again, it's for the newest Appropriate Technology group. This time, it will be held near San Pedro Jocopilas, Anthony's site just outside of Quiché. Everyone except Anthony will sleep in a hotel in Quiché. Two thirds of the new trainees are females. Since the nature of the Appropriate Technology program has changed, they will work primarily as health promoters in conjunction with local health centers. The building projects we will concentrate on this week will seem increasingly irrelevant as these neophytes spend more time in country.

JUNE 9, 2008

Tonight I will watch *Blood Diamond*; this afternoon, I bought the pirated DVD at the Nebaj market for 15Q. I will eat another pasta dinner alone tonight, listening to the steady patter of the rain. I cannot imagine a stint in the Peace Corps without pasta, or solitude for that matter. I have grown to love Nebaj even though I am ready for a change. I need to move on. I need a fresh start. There are not enough eligible young women for me in this town anyway. Right now Athens, Georgia, looks like paradise; game days on north campus were elysian, flirting with intelligent girls and drinking good bourbon. I will never be able to get enough of that.

JUNE 16, 2008

The first day with Engineers Without Borders in Quejchip was a wild one. Most of them happen to be students at the University of Wisconsin-Milwaukee. We are surveying the conduction line for a second time, mostly for fun, when we are attacked by bees. Luckily, no one is stung more than three or four times. Normally, groups like this come to Guatemala with tons of theoretical knowledge about civil engineering and hydraulics, yet few have much practical experience. By the time they leave, many will realize that 80 percent of what they learn in the classroom is irrelevant, impractical, or too complicated. This group is no exception.

JUNE 18, 2008

My friend James Schintz and I are doing our Close of Service medical exams concurrently this week. James has worked in a town near Xela called San Martín for the past two years. Specifically, he was an adviser at a savings-and-loan cooperative there. James and I will each have a full day of medical examinations and doctor visits. But that is for the first day. The other two days will be more laid-back. On those days, we'll just need to crap in a cup and drop our respective stool samples off at a lab in Antigua or

Guatemala City. Another stipulation is the tuberculosis skin test; we'll each need to return to the medical office two days after the TB test was administered. This is a quick process, since the nurse will just glance at our arms and then sign a couple documents. If either of us has TB, we'll both know it within the next twenty-four hours. For a positive test, a small portion of the skin on the person's forearm would be irritated, usually resulting in redness and elevation near the injection site. Typically, the skin starts to rise within the first twelve hours of the exam and continues to do so for several days thereafter.

Last night, we went out for a few drinks; a few quickly turned into a dozen or more. We spent most of the evening at Mono Loco. We were reminiscing about our time in Guatemala. Today Johanna, one of the Peace Corps nurses, tells both of us that we reek of alcohol … at around noon. Of course, we were perfectly sober. We just smell like cheap rum. Thereafter, we try to keep a low profile and leave the training center without being noticed. Unfortunately, James and I run into Peace Corps Country Director Jim Adriance, and later, on our way out, my APCD, Basilio Estrada. We act so awkward that both of them probably assume we are stoned. There is nothing like finishing on a high note.

JUNE 26, 2008

I am glad to be back in Nebaj for a few days, in spite of the relentless rain. Things are going moderately well with the Engineers Without Borders folks. However, two people have flown home early, which is absurd since they were only here for ten days. They claimed that they were too sick to stay. That's ridiculous. They just couldn't take it. A lot of things that people take for granted in the Peace Corps are not to be taken for granted, or so I have come to believe. This evening, I go out for beers at the pool hall with the group. Good times are had by all.

JULY 9, 2008

I have only two weeks left in Nebaj. My job as a PCV, for all intents and purposes, is over. I just need to write a couple of reports for bureaucrats in Guatemala City and DC. I am leaving in August. I am leaving and not coming back for at least several months, maybe even years. I am leaving this life behind. But is that really what I am doing? Or will I be taking this life and these lessons with me wherever I go? The latter of the two suppositions seems more likely. Guatemala, what have you done to me? You will not, you cannot let my subconscious rest in peace. It has happened: Guatemala has become my "moveable feast." My perception of reality is forever altered; I interpret the world differently. And I am not alone. I should stop lying to myself and admit that I would prefer nothing else.

JULY 13, 2008: COTZAL

As previously stated, two of the Agua Para la Salud masons, Antonio Cavinal and his son Juan, were born and raised in Cotzal. I am in Cotzal for the weekend visiting my friend Josh Kyller, but I also plan on spending some time with Antonio. I will be leaving the country in less than a month. I can always communicate with Josh via e-mail or cell phone. It will be much harder to stay in touch with Antonio. He has asked me to meet him near his house. Upon arrival, I quickly realize that Antonio lives in a sketchy part of town.

I see a couple of Guatemalans smoking a joint inside the cantina. The owner has not even raised an eyebrow. I am no stranger to Guatemalan cantinas and basic cantina etiquette, but this is unheard of in rural Guatemala. That leaves no doubt in my mind. They are gang members. I quickly text Josh, and he advises me to be careful. I realize that I should walk back to Josh's house immediately. But I am too curious to succumb to reason at this point; this afternoon could be a priceless sociological study. I decide to stay.

I still can't believe that Antonio has been hanging out with these guys all morning. Antonio admits that they are in a gang— Dieciocho (The number "eighteen" in English)—and that the two guys are friends of his, since they live near him. He buys me a beer and tells me not to worry. I comply. I am following Antonio's lead now.

We spend the next several hours with these two guys; Josh has a community basketball game to participate in, so he isn't around. I realize after about an hour that they are both carrying guns. I don't ask if they are loaded or not. I'm sure they are. Twenty-one-year-old Domingo, the older of the two, asks me if I would be interested in helping him with some business. Evidently, nobody can afford weed in Cotzal. He tells me that he is looking to build up contacts around the lake and in the Antigua-Guatemala City area. We trade phone numbers, but I'll never call the guy. I do this because I don't want to offend him. I will be leaving the country in less than a month, so I figure it doesn't really matter.

JULY 20, 2008

I have just given all the kids at El Descanso a loaf of Don's banana bread. Lupita could not have been happier when I arrived with her apple pie this afternoon. I gave Juana, the server at Lupita's, a loaf of Don's banana bread as well. Preparing to leave is emotional. I feel unstable, confused, and nostalgic in some unclear way.

If my past transgressions were not enough, this will be. It's official: Any hope I had for a career in politics has ended today. I confess. I slaughtered a rabbit this afternoon. I hadn't planned on being the guy, but no one else wanted to do it. Chris, Peter, and Josh and his girlfriend Natalie were all there. All of them had been thrilled about participating in the purchase of the animal for 35Q at Don's. Their enthusiasm waned precipitously when we got back to my house. None of them would do it. I had to hit the little guy over the head with a piece of wood three times to kill the poor fella—not good. Peter got pictures of the entire thing. Then Josh and I had to clean the animal. His skin came off just like a sweater. Then I ripped his guts out and threw them on some pieces of newspaper. After applying olive oil, salt, and pepper liberally, we threw Bugs in the oven with some carrots and potatoes. We had an okay dinner, but not an excellent one. Rabbit is nowhere near as tasty as chicken; the meat is just too tough.

JULY 31, 2008

I just got back from a great trip to Chiapas with Josh and a few other PCVs from Josh's training group. Reality has just hit me; I am no longer a Peace Corps volunteer. I have seen this moment coming for years, but the change still feels abrupt. Like the blink of an eye, the life I lived, loved, and at times hated in Guatemala is gone forever. The Peace Corps has certainly stirred up some contradictory feelings. Encapsulating two years in Nebaj is tough; revisiting my Peace Corps journey is impossible. Nevertheless, I know the time to get out is now. I must move on and continue to grow as a person. I will embrace home with guarded optimism. I will soon be an RPCV, a Returned Peace Corps volunteer, one more chapter in the annals of Peace Corps history.

AUGUST 1, 2008

Tonight will be my last in Nebaj. I have been taking Tylenol PM to get to sleep these past few days. I am so anxious and excited and confused and sad about leaving. This plethora of emotions is driving me crazy. Being a human can be complicated; right now, I'm too exhausted to dwell any longer on the subject.

I have said good-bye to all my Peace Corps friends in person or on the phone. In Nebaj, I have said good-bye to everyone except Lupita, Don, and Lynn. Peter and I will have breakfast with Lynn in a couple of days on the lake. Today Diego, Pedro, and Antonio all brought some nice handmade gifts to the house—exactly what I had been hoping for. I am listening to Dylan's "Forever Young" as I write, trying to find some inner peace as I prepare to leave. I know that joining the Peace Corps was a good decision. Looking myself in the mirror has never been easier. At the end of the day, helping people has taught me so much about life. Leaving Nebaj feels eerily like leaving Athens, Georgia, in the winter of 2005. The only difference is the unquestionable singularity of the Peace Corps experience. Hundreds of thousands, probably even millions of people, graduated from a four-year university this summer. Only a few thousand at the most can say they successfully completed a twenty-seven-month stint in the Peace Corps.

Just as I rode with former site mate Kelsi Black on her last ride from Nebaj to Quiché in November 2006, Peter will accompany me on my last trip from Nebaj down to Quiché tomorrow. We will stop off in San Pedro la Laguna and then spend a couple of days in Antigua.

AUGUST 6, 2008: THE HOMECOMING

I fly home in a few hours to celebrate my mom's fifty-fourth birthday. I have a late night that won't end until I find my seat on the plane. Ana Lucrecia, my host mom from training, cried when I hugged her for the last time yesterday. I thought that her behavior was excessively sentimental at the time, but now I am not so sure. It's 4:50 a.m. Tears have started to well in my eyes. I have stayed up all night with James, his girlfriend Lou, and Peter. We are restlessly waiting on the curb at James' new apartment in Antigua. My shuttle should arrive at 5:00 a.m. A grey van rounds the corner as we listen to Julieta Venega's "Me Voy" for the third consecutive time. I ambivalently accept the fact that this will be the last time I see Guatemala for a long time. I cry at the Guatemala City airport, and again when I land in Dallas.

EPILOGUE

*"We shall not cease from exploration and the end of
all our exploring will be to arrive where we started
and to know the place for the first time."*

—*T. S. Eliot*

FIESTA OF SUNSET: PEACE CORPS REFLECTIONS

I am in the middle of final exams, trying to make sense of producer
theory, market externalities, and wondering how the rise of China
will alter the current international order. I am surrounded by
impressive classmates who come from all corners of the globe and
bring with them a myriad of experience. I live in New York City,
a place of unsurpassed vibrancy and diversity. I still can't believe
I got accepted to Columbia; my GPA as an undergraduate was
an unimpressive 2.94. I have plenty of work to do, but I cannot
concentrate. I am returning to Guatemala for a wedding in less
than three weeks.

Some of life's experiences are difficult to verbalize; those
moments just linger on the periphery of conventional language. I
know that my time in the Peace Corps may seem incomprehensible
or esoteric to many people. For me, poverty and illiteracy used to

be distant, boring concepts—like Sanskrit, calculus, or dieting. I know that even fewer people will understand or care.

Spending two years in an indigenous village taught me that idealistic individuals can effect change. I have learned that dedication, honesty, hard work, and courage are the principles upon which that change can be created, no matter how farfetched or implausible those ideas might seem. I have witnessed incredible acts of altruism firsthand, both on the part of Americans and Guatemalans. But I have also seen the negative—waste, fraud, negligence, corruption, laziness, indifference, dishonesty, and more.

As a child, I grew up in a wealthy neighborhood of Dallas. I was spoiled. All my former classmates and I obliviously took our socioeconomic situation for granted. We assumed that clean drinking water and a good school system were closer to the status quo than the exception. We knew we would all go to college after high school, because that was only natural. Even today, I can confidently assume that few of my former classmates have ever worked or volunteered in a developing country since we graduated nearly a decade ago.

Many Americans fail to understand how lucky they are. Most will acknowledge global inequality but do nothing to alleviate it. Others will speak about fighting poverty and economic disparities with their money. And yes, money certainly is a necessary part of the equation. But few are willing to take a greater risk by giving a part of themselves. That risk is never as daunting as it may at first appear. My story is a case in point. I was once a coward.

Several weeks ago, I volunteered at Columbia's Career Fair for International Organizations. I sat at the Peace Corps table all day. I answered dozens of thoughtful questions and discussed my service working for a local NGO in Guatemala. I was happy to help; those fears and anxieties that potential Peace Corps applicants harbor were once my own. I still consider myself an intensely private person, usually afraid to share my innermost thoughts and feelings. Now I am motivated by another kind of fear. I feel compelled to share what I have learned and done. Because if I do not, I am afraid that it may soon be forgotten.

Those twenty-seven months truly were the adventure of a lifetime. I made lasting friendships and helped some people, but I understand that I got more out of it than I could have ever put in. Most importantly, I will never let fear and doubt control my life.

I am only one person, and I am deeply flawed. I was a mean older brother. I could never commit to a relationship. I only picked the fights I knew I could win. I supported the invasion of Iraq. I even used to consider myself a Republican. But I am a human being, and redemption is possible. I have chosen life. Recovery starts with acceptance. This is the end of one part, not the whole story. Maybe this is "the fiesta of sunset" that Neruda spoke of in *Clenched Soul*. My classmates and I are not finished. People do not study economic and political development at Columbia's School of International and Public Affairs (SIPA) so that they can sit behind a desk and push paper for thirty years. I am surrounded by men and women of action, many of whom are professors at SIPA.

Though global poverty statistics vary, some things are clear. Billions of people live on less than two dollars per day. Malnutrition, illiteracy, gender inequality, and infant mortality are still prevalent in the developing world. And climate change isn't helping. There will be no shortage of problems to address when we graduate. "Everything passes, only the truth remains." Dostoyevsky was right. Maybe I should start drinking more vodka.

The End

ACKNOWLEDGMENTS

I want to thank friends and family who provided me with excellent suggestions on various versions of this manuscript. I am very thankful that the following people are part of my life: Brannon Albritton, Ben Coffee, Brady Evans, Blake Smith, Alex Jarman, Brian Finnerty, Mario Cambardella, Owen Gray, Doug Andres, John Wiley, Baber Allen, Steve Pack, Steve Rebillot, Kyle Giddens, Jim Livingston, M. Gibson Rainwater and Stephen Clayton.

Former Peace Corps Country Director Todd Sloan and former Interim Country Director James Adriance are good men and fine leaders. Ana Luisa, Kathy, and Johanna in the Peace Corps medical office are tremendous assets to Peace Corps Guatemala. The same can be said for Peace Corps Trainer David Castillo and Training Director Craig Badger.

Lynn Roberts was more of a father figure than a supervisor when I lived in Guatemala; he continues to inspire me. The masons at Agua Para la Salud are some of the most talented and tireless people I've ever been around. In Nebaj, they took me under their wing and treated me like one of their own.

Most significantly, I want to thank some of the other Peace Corps volunteers that I connected with during my service. My experience would not have been the same without them. This list includes but is not limited to: Anthony Hicks, Stephanie

Kollar, Andrew Gall, Josh Kyller, Chris Mullen, Gwen Kernan, Michael Breslin, Cecelia Paredes, Holly Bonetti, Kody Gerkin, Carin Robinson, J. P. Gibbons, Eric Schroeder, James Schintz, Rob Krieger, Jennifer Slotnik, Meghan Curran, Liam Lunstrum, and B. J. Osorio. And while he never officially worked for the Peace Corps, I am especially grateful to Peter Cruddas for all his encouragement with this book and, more importantly, for his friendship. As J. R. R. Tolkien once said, "Not all those who wander are lost."

CPSIA information can be obtained at www.ICGtesting.com
Printed in the USA
LVOW081207231011

251691LV00002B/89/P